The

BURNING

WITHIN

THE
BURNING
WITHIN

RANELLE
WALLACE

WITH
CURTIS TAYLOR

GOLD LEAF PRESS

The Burning Within
© 1994 by RaNelle Wallace
All rights reserved
Printed in the United States of America

No portion of this book may be reproduced in any form
without written permission from the publisher,
Gold Leaf Press, 2533 North Carson St., Suite 1544,
Carson City, NV 89706

Library of Congress Cataloging-in-Publication Data

Wallace, RaNelle
The burning within
p.   cm.
ISBN 1-882723-05-8
1. Wallace, RaNelle. 2. Burns and scalds—Patients—
United States—Biography. I. Taylor, Curtis. II. Title.
RD96.4.W335A3   1994
362.1'9711092—dc20
[B]   94-260

10 9 8 7 6 5 4 3 2 1

DEDICATION

THIS BOOK IS DEDICATED TO MY FATHER IN HEAVEN AND TO the Savior who refined me in fire. To my husband, Terry, and to my children whose love inspires and sustains me and whose patience saw me through the completion of this book. To my father and mother, extended family, and friends whose hands have always reached out to bring me into the light and to lift me up. And finally, to my grandmother who taught me the great power of love; who stands as a reminder of God's love; and who wants me to share this message of love with everyone. For this purpose this book has come to pass.

ACKNOWLEDGEMENTS

THIS BOOK IS A TESTAMENT OF THE SUSTAINING INSPIRATION, unselfish service, support, faith, and love that many people have given me. No words could express the great love and gratitude that fills my heart.

A special thanks and dedication to Bob and Patty who remind me always that people do triumph over tragedy; to Dr. Grossman and Dr. Saffel and the other doctors, nurses and therapists whose skillful talents gave me life and hope; to friends and strangers from all walks of life and from different faiths whose prayers, concern, and support were a strong factor in my healing; and to all those who contributed to my trust fund—they gave more than money, they gave love—and to Steve for administrating the fund.

Thank you to the people of Bakersfield for bringing my story and its message to the world, and to Betty Eadie for bringing my story to Gold Leaf Press and for her love and support.

Many thanks go to the people who were part of my story but are not mentioned in this book—I hold these friends and family members in great esteem! And thanks to everyone who kept pushing me to write this book.

I am indebted to writer Marilyn Brown and editor Darla Isackson. Marilyn spent months organizing and refining my story from tape transcripts and Darla, of Gold Leaf Press, gave sense and direction to this work. The book is stronger for the efforts of these talented women.

A very special thanks to Curtis Taylor who reached into my heart and mind and, in beautiful, powerful writing, brought to paper what I could not express. Thank you, Curtis, for having the spiritual strength to endure your own trials and sacrifices in order to see this book through. Thank you for giving me the love and support of a truly great friend and for being so in tune with the Lord. You are very talented, Curtis, not just in your writing, but in all that you give to the world. The world is a better place because you're in it.

I would like to thank my husband, Terry, who is a GREAT MAN because he had the courage to let the truth be told. You have given me the strength to bear my burdens and have always loved me in spite of me. You have brought me to a higher understanding of what love really is. Terry, we were truly meant to be together. I am proud to be your wife.

Chapter

O N E

I STOOD ON THE TARMAC AT THE SALT LAKE CITY AIRPORT and nervously looked south. The horizon was a flat deck of unbroken clouds so low and thick that I couldn't tell where the ground ended and the clouds began. But they didn't look like storm clouds. I had seen clouds like this rolling in from the ocean in southern California—heavy but harmless clouds that gave a spattering of rain, a blast of wind, and then moved on. I was relieved that these weren't more menacing, but while I helped Terry, my husband, load the plane, I felt the air growing cooler, sharper with the growing light, not warmer.

I felt that something terrible was about to happen. The premonition came to me in a wave of fear that left me quaking. I had felt the warning for weeks but had refused to follow it. Now I was afraid it might be too late.

"Terry, I think we ought to be leaving right away," I said. "It's getting colder."

"I told you the weather service thinks it's okay," he said. "I called just before we left." He stood up and faced the ceiling of clouds toward the south in the direction of our flight path, and braced himself against a sudden frigid gust. "Yeah, I guess we should hurry," he agreed as he zipped his jacket and went back to packing. When the weight was as evenly distributed as we could get it, Terry went around the plane checking all the movable parts and electrical connections. We were ready. The plane was already fueled, and a minute or two later we were into our safety check. Everything cleared—no problems—and Terry revved the engine.

Suddenly I remembered something. Our door had a nasty habit of popping open during flight. I pushed it open and banged it shut. I tested it, and the door seemed under control—for now. The propeller blurred to life and slowly pulled us down the runway.

Terry and I said as little as possible. We had taken time off for this trip together, to find out if we still loved each other enough to remain husband and wife—a team that could pull together and sacrifice for one another. The answer was now as obvious as the dull, slate sky in front of us. Utah had been a wonderland of fantasy and denial. Now we were heading back to the demands of unyielding fact and truth. We were to confront the monster of wrenching our family in two and going our separate ways.

We rose into the sky with about 1,500 feet clearance between the clouds and the ground, plenty of room to fly, and we turned slightly west to get out over the desert. We picked up the VOR signal coming out of Delta, about a hundred miles south, and turned toward it. The VOR is a high-frequency radio beacon for pilots. All we had to do was follow it until we picked up another signal coming out of Las Vegas. By then, according to the forecasters, the worst weather would be behind us.

The monotonous roar of the engine filled the cockpit as we headed for the point where the clouds and earth merged, though I couldn't tell exactly where that was.

Our plane was a V-tail Bonanza, a type not known for stability in flight. V-tails can be smooth, sleek fliers in calm weather, but because of their lack of a true vertical stabilizer, they tend to yaw, or fishtail, in strong winds. It's not something you have to worry about as long as you avoid severe turbulence. Things can get tricky if you go into a storm or into clouds, and I noticed we were doing both. The closer we got to the point where earth seemed to be touching sky, the stronger the winds became and the lower we had to fly to stay below the clouds. Either the ceiling was lowering as we went, or the terrain was rising. Terry pulled back on the stick to let us rise a little, and a blinding flash of lightning filled the cabin. The plane rattled and shook with the explosion of thunder, and we fishtailed through the sky for a heart-stopping moment before Terry managed to pull us straight.

I looked out my window to see where the lightning had hit the ground. A reddish glow was forming in a large clump of brush down to my right. "Look, it's started a fire down there," I managed to say. I turned back to Terry. His knuckles were white on the stick. We were literally in the middle of nowhere, no towns below us, no roads, no horizon in front of us, no discernable line of sky, no color, no definition—nothing. Lightning could hit us now and throw us out of the air, and nobody would even know where to start looking for us. We were so low that the radar back in Salt Lake was certainly unable to see us. We had been swallowed up by an awesome grayness, a maw of desert and cloud.

Lightning shot out of the clouds again, further off to the right, and we waited for the shock wave. Either we didn't feel it, or it blended with the turbulence that was bouncing us around. Terry yelled that he thought we might be able to get above the clouds if they were low enough, and he pulled back on the stick again. We pulled sharply up, and our windshield was suddenly blanketed with mist and rain. Where just a moment before we had been so close to the ground that we could see sagebrush and earth for a mile all around, now we could see nothing. We were totally blind. Almost instantly I noticed a drop in temperature, and the plane began rattling violently. We fishtailed again, and Terry and I were thrown from side to side in our seats. He fought for control, but the buffeting was so strong he could hardly keep the plane straight. The cabin was getting unbelievably cold. I checked the heater switch and found it was on high. There was nothing more we could do; the freezing winds were surging through every crevice in the craft.

Terry said a single word, and my spine chilled.

"Ice."

I looked up and saw a layer of ice forming before my eyes on the windshield. The surface temperature of the plane was colder than the surrounding air, and it was acting like a freezer coil in the mist and rain. If the wings iced up, we wouldn't have to worry about lightning much longer; we'd lose our lift and plunge like a rock to the earth. Terry pushed the stick forward to try to get us back down out of the clouds, but there was no bottom to the clouds. We kept descending, and for an agonizing second or two we watched the altimeter, then the windshield, then the altimeter, then the windshield looking for the earth. When I thought that we would plow into the ground, Terry pulled back on the stick and we veered up. We never did see the ground or know how close our belly had come to it. All we knew, as we looked at the map, was that the contour markings showed the elevation rising the farther south we went. The eleven-thousand-foot peaks of the Wasatch Front were still forty or fifty miles off to our left, but other, smaller peaks jutted up from valley floors all around us. We not only had to avoid flying into the ground, as we may have almost done, but we had to avoid the occasional mountain that might suddenly appear right in front of us.

Terry didn't know how to fly by instruments alone. Although he had meant to get his instrument rating a few months back, and had studied for it, he hadn't flown by them before. We could watch the altimeter and the false horizon on the console and check our direction on the compass, but we were really flying blind—at about 130 miles per hour. Suddenly my stomach knotted as the realization hit me that each second, each fraction of a second, might be my last. A mountain could be ten feet in front of us, and we wouldn't see it. I caught myself holding my breath, waiting—for what? I stared out the icy windshield and tried to see the end coming.

We were still bouncing up and down and side to side, and the plane was rattling and groaning like it would fall apart any second. But we kept flying. It wasn't as if we were in a car and could just pull over and wait out the storm; we had to keep going, to try to find some clear air just beneath the clouds again—if there was any. The plane jolted sharply, and I felt a sudden change in air pressure. Wind started screaming in my right ear, and my entire right side was pelted with rain and slush. How was the rain getting in? I looked to the right and saw that the door had popped open. Terrified, I grabbed the handle, trying to shut the door as much as possible.

"Let's land!" I yelled over the rushing air.

Terry's lips were drawn tight as he looked straight ahead. He shook his head no.

"Come on, Terry! Get serious. I can't hold this door forever. We've got to land!" Snow was swirling into the cockpit around my legs and feet. My hand stung, and I looked at it. I couldn't see anything at first, but then it stung again. Splinters of ice were shooting into my wrist and hand at 130 miles per hour. Small cuts began showing red. "Terry! Take us down. I can't hold on any longer!"

"No," he said. "You've got to hold on until we get to St. George."

I couldn't believe what he was saying. St. George was a hundred miles away—if we were even going in the right direction. I would no more make it to St. George than I would to the North Pole. "We can't do this!" I screamed. "The weather's getting worse. We can't keep going!"

Terry looked over, staring at me for a moment. "Where are we going to land?" he asked. "Do you see anywhere?"

"Take it down!" I yelled. "We've got to land!"

Tentatively at first, Terry moved the stick forward, and we began inching down. He pushed it a little further, and our rate of descent increased. We watched the altimeter again. Fifty-five hundred feet. Still snow and ice and fog all around. The plane jumped up and down, dancing in the confused winds. Fifty-four hundred feet. Fifty-three hundred feet. The maps showed the altitude of the land here—depending on where we were—at about five thousand feet. Our attention focused again on the altimeter and windshield. Where was the ground? Fifty-two hundred feet. If we were going to see the ground before we felt it, it was going to happen right away. Fifty-one hundred. Still nothing but ice and fog. Five thousand feet. Where were we? We should have *hit* ground by now. Forty-nine hundred. Forty-eight hundred. This was impossible. Our maps said we were near Fillmore, which is right at five thousand feet. Suddenly Terry jerked and banked the plane to my side. I screamed and I held the door as the plane tilted over me.

"What are you doing?" I yelled.

"I saw something!" he called over the roar in the cockpit. "A truck or something. I'm going back."

I was looking right out the open door and didn't see anything but frozen mist and red cuts on my arm. We circled and pulled in a little lower, then a little lower still. I held my breath and waited for the impact of earth and plane. "There it is!" he yelled. "Look!"

A bulldozer was sitting on a dirt road, not a hundred feet below us. The clouds cleared a little as we came out of them. The tufts of sage lining the narrow dirt strip were the most welcome sight I had ever seen. Then it was gone. We were back in the enveloping mist, and I could feel ice driving into my wrist again. It was as if we had been covered by a huge blanket, blinding us. There was nothing we could do. When another hole appeared in the mist, Terry threw the stick forward and darted down through it. The tractor and the road came back into view off to our right side. We were going to make it! I heard the groan of the landing gear coming down and the click-click as it locked into place.

Landing on asphalt is difficult enough in a small plane, but landing on dirt is totally different. Terry had nearly killed us once landing on a dirt airfield. He had over-braked, causing the plane to slide sideways, pulling us to within inches of a tree. But since then he had practiced and knew how to work the pedals just right to prepare for the sudden stop. We were fifteen feet above the ground, and the crosswind was toying with us, popping us up and down, sliding us to the left then to the right. We were ten feet above the ground, and we could see large puddles of mud racing beneath us. Now we knew why the tractor was working on the road; it would take a four-wheel drive vehicle to negotiate it. I held my

breath, and suddenly the nose reared up and we banked hard
to the right.

"I can't do it!" Terry yelled.

I was looking out the open door straight at the ground. I
was so close I could have jumped out. I held the handle for
all I was worth. A small juniper tree came out of nowhere—
and I prayed we would miss it. But a sudden gust of wind
pushed us to the right, tilting my side down, and I heard an
ugly ripping sound as our right wing sheared through the top
of the tree. Our tail slipped out behind us to the left, and our
speed decreased immediately. I thought we were going to stall
or spin sideways through the air until we dropped. Terry's
hands and feet worked the controls feverishly, straining at the
flaps and elevators, then working the rudders to pull the tail
back behind us. He was able to soften our turn; then using
the flaps and elevators again, he increased the angle of attack
and hit the throttle to give it all the power our little 1946 V-
tail could muster. The engine gave an agonizing groan, and I
prayed that the wind would die just a little so we could pull
our right wing up. The plane jerked, and suddenly we were
twenty feet off the ground, then thirty, then fifty, and I knew
we would make it. Winds still buffeted the plane, flinging
Terry and me from side to side, testing the strength of our
seat belts. And somehow I still had hold of the door.

"Dear God," I said out loud, "get me through this. Please
get me down, and I swear, I promise, I will listen to your
warnings from now on. I will do *anything*, but please, please
get us through this."

"Hold on to that door!" Terry yelled.

"Get us down!" I yelled.

"I can't! There are too many potholes. We'd somersault."

"Terry, get this plane down! Now!"

"I can't. We'll crash!"

I started praying again, promising, swearing, vowing that I would never fly again if He would just get us down. We were skimming through a fairly clear sky just below the clouds and a hundred feet above the ground. A hundred feet of clear sky to fly in is like a six-foot wide lane to drive a car in; one mistake and you're dead.

"How does the wing look?" Terry asked.

I had already checked it after hitting the tree. "It's okay," I said. "Nothing's broken off."

We flew a few more miles, me praying fervently out loud, Terry fighting the stick and pedals for control in the wind. We came over a little rise, and right before us lay a perfect asphalt runway.

Terry lowered the landing gear again and lined up the plane. I couldn't believe it. Somebody had put a beautiful little landing strip right in front of us. Of course I had no idea where we were, but at the moment I didn't want to be anywhere else in the world.

"Thank you, thank you, thank you," I repeated out loud, tears coming to my eyes.

"RaNelle, we're going to touch down!" Terry yelled. "You pull the door shut. I'll try to get down to about thirty miles an hour."

Touch down! Did I hear him right? I turned and looked at him.

"Just pull it closed when we touch down!" he yelled. "We need to get out of here—and get home."

I must have reddened like a stop light. "Are you crazy! Get this thing on the ground and stop—Now!"

"No, slam the door, and we'll take off. We need to get home."

I lined up my choices. I could try to convince him to stop the plane, or I could use some stratagem, such as hitting him over the head with a crowbar. Or I could submit to his plan and die with him up against the side of some mountain. Unfortunately, the crowbar was not available—I would have to think of something else.

As we approached the runway, the landing looked simple enough. Three thousand feet of flat asphalt stretched ahead. But as we touched down, the plane swung dizzily to the left on invisible ice, and I was overcome by vertigo. Terrified, I held on to the door as firmly as I could while Terry worked the rudder to correct our tail as we skidded along at nearly a hundred miles an hour. I was petrified. He had done an amazing job of flying all day, but skidding sideways down the runway was the last straw. Terry's reign in the plane was about to end. I decided it was time to stop flying. We were going to ground ourselves for a long time.

Finally, Terry regained control and brought us true again. We slowed. "Okay, RaNelle, get ready!" he shouted over the propeller noise.

I said nothing.

We slowed to forty miles an hour, then thirty.

"Okay, try it now!"

I held the door in place.

"Now, RaNelle, now!" he yelled as we slowed further.

I was a statue, eyes straight ahead, silent.

"Close the door!" he screamed. "Slam it! Slam it!" We couldn't have been going more than ten miles an hour now, maybe five. I unlatched my seat belt, swiveled to the right and kicked the door all the way open. Then I jumped out on the wing and a moment later I was on the ground.

"What are you doing?" Terry yelled, and I started walking

forward, heading for a low, drab-looking building about a hundred yards away. Terry taxied alongside me, ordering me, pleading for me to get in.

I knew, I mean I *absolutely knew,* that we had just been saved by a miracle. I knew that Deity had heard my prayer and offered us this perfect little runway, and the last thing I was going to do was say thanks, get back in the plane, and take off for the wild gray yonder. Terry had to be crazy if he thought I was going do that. In fact, he *was* crazy. I had proof. Anybody would have thought so right then—him taxiing alongside me, trying to talk me into committing suicide with him.

"What do you think you're doing?" he yelled.

"I'm walking."

"Where?"

"I'm walking home."

"What! Are you serious? Get in here!"

"No way!"

The engine roared, and for a second I thought he might take off without me. Fine. Let him go crash and burn on his own.

"Get back in here!" he said. "You can't walk to California."

"You're right," I said. "I'll hitchhike."

He killed the engine and moments later he came out the door—the one that never stayed shut when it was supposed to—and ran down the wing. Moments later he was beside me. "RaNelle," he said, struggling to be calm. "There's nobody out here. It's deserted. We don't even know where we are."

"I know where I am. I'm on the ground. And that's where I'm staying. I mean it, Terry, I am not getting in that plane again. There's nothing you can do to get me back in there."

"RaNelle, you're not being reasonable. You could die here."

I had just been placed on the ground by an act of God, and Terry thought that staying there was unreasonable. How had I lived with him as long as I had?

"There's nowhere to stay here," he went on. When Terry wanted something, he wanted it all the way. No fooling around, no playing games, no giving in when the whole world—and God—told him to *Stop.* "Look," he said, "it's stopped raining. Let's get back in the plane."

He was right about that; it had stopped raining, or snowing, or sleeting, or whatever it had been doing, but there was no way I was getting in that plane. We were at the building now, and I started looking for a way to get in. I was about to break a window when I heard the sound of a truck. We looked around the corner and saw a white, beat-up, 1960s pickup heading right for us. It came to a stop, and a man in his early forties got out and walked over to us. He wore a faded blue shirt, suspenders, old jeans, and cowboy boots.

"'S'thar a problem?" he inquired in some sort of drawl that I had never heard before.

I eyed him carefully. He looked like a farmer. "Where are we?" I asked.

"Why," he said in a drawn-out tone that lasted about twice as long as it needed to, "yer'n Dale-ta."

"We're in what?"

He looked at me funny for a moment. "Your'n Dale-ta."

"Oh, Delta," I said. Delta was about thirty miles west of Fillmore. And it did seem to be in the bottom of a broad valley, probably two or three hundred feet below Fillmore. Then I realized that the VOR came from right here! It came from this airport. We were literally on top of it.

"What kin uh do fer ya?" the man asked. He was being very kind, but I couldn't understand all of his words. I noticed that he kept a close eye on Terry, who stood quietly at my side, obviously disgusted.

"Is there a hotel near here?" I asked.

"Yup, there is," he replied evenly, still watching Terry. "We have one hotel in town."

"Well, I hate to impose on you, but could you take me there?"

The "me" in the sentence must have caught his attention, but he didn't show it. He just kept an eye on Terry and said, "Be pleased to."

I told him I would get my luggage, and I turned to walk back to the plane.

This was it. As far as I was concerned, Terry could fly to Las Vegas or home to Bakersfield or anywhere he wanted. I was leaving him—now. Or maybe he was leaving me. I held my breath, expecting to hear footsteps.

They came soon enough and Terry was now walking beside me.

We didn't speak as we approached the plane, but as he started pulling out the luggage I noticed that his bags were coming out too. He wasn't leaving. *What does it take?* I thought. We don't care for each other; we don't even like each other. Why doesn't he just get in that plane and let go?

We got in the truck and drove toward Delta, just a few miles away. Almost immediately I was jabbering away like a bird. Everything that had just happened came spilling out of me like a torrent. I couldn't turn it off, and the farmer heard it all: the door popping open, the ice, flying blind in the clouds, hitting the juniper—which, thankfully, hadn't damaged the wing—and then finding the airport at just the right time. The farmer must have thought I was crazy, which would have been a true assessment at that moment, but he occasionally nodded his head and said, "Yup." My mouth was like a race car that couldn't be stopped. My adrenaline was flowing, and the more he said "Yup," the more I had to tell him. By the time we pulled up to the hotel he had heard everything at least twice, and I was starting to remember more. Terry was silent.

After we thanked him and offered him money, which he wouldn't take, we said good-bye. He eyed Terry once more, then looked at me and said, "Yup." Then he climbed back in his old white truck and drove away.

We went into the hotel—the smallest I had ever seen—and were greeted by a sweet-looking woman. She politely explained that the hotel was full, and suddenly my energy took an evil turn.

"Full!" I exploded, already embarrassed at what I was doing. "What's the population here?"

"What?" she said, startled.

"What's the population here?"

"Well, a couple thousand, I suppose."

"So, is this what they all do—check themselves into the only hotel in town? Isn't there anything else for them to do around here?"

She was taken aback, but I didn't care. I was like a bear on the attack, all my energy focused on the miserable situation I was in.

I turned my anger on Terry next. "What are we going to do, Terry?" I asked—as if I really wanted to hear from him. Fortunately, he didn't answer. "Here we are, stuck in Delta, Utah," I bellowed. "And I can tell you right now I'm not spending the night on this lobby floor. So *what* are we going to do?" I glared at the woman and Terry, daring either of them to answer. Finally she spoke.

"You could go to the movie down the street," she said cautiously. "Sometimes our customers don't show up for their reservations, and after six I can cancel one of them and give you a room."

The sweetness in her voice should have broken through my anger, but I was livid. I couldn't account for the rage I felt. She stepped around the desk and suggested that we leave our luggage with her and find the movie theater around the corner. What could I do? We left our luggage and walked down the street to the theater. The afternoon matinee was just starting, so we bought tickets and went in.

The theater was big enough, maybe, for an afternoon Grange meeting, but not for a movie, and people were sitting on *folding* chairs. Without padding. They were crammed together like the room was meant more for a religious revival than for a movie. The projector started up behind us like a Sherman tank revving its engine, and I just stood in the aisle, flabbergasted. The projector clicked along, actually not so much like a Sherman tank, but like a couple of playing cards flipping along in a bicycle wheel. The rat-tat-tat-tat was already driving me crazy. I stood in the aisle, watching the opening credits and searching my mind for an appropriate invective to christen this moment with. Terry suggested we take a seat, any seat, and sit down. I honestly couldn't think of words to say, and before I knew it I was sitting on the hardest, slipperiest chair I had ever sat on, watching a wilderness film that had to have been made before the projector itself was.

My mind whirled in frustration and disbelief. We had actually paid for this opportunity. We had flown to Delta,

Utah, gone to a theater, and laid down seven or eight bucks to get in. What was happening to my life? I wasn't thinking about miracles now, about planes being led out of the sky to perfect little landing strips in the middle of nowhere. I was thinking about the ugly situation I had made for myself, about the emptiness in my heart, about my children, Christina and Jason, who were staying with my mother, and about the destruction my three- and one-year-old were no doubt inflicting on her house that very moment. She had called the day before, and I heard something break in the background, a solid, meaty crash that took my mother's breath away—and mine—and then I heard my mother saying, "*Please*, RaNelle, come home soon." And I thought about Terry and his stubbornness that had nearly caused our deaths. The cost of staying together was now too great, I realized. Our lives had been close to ruin for too long. In fact, I was almost glad we were splitting up.

The film flickered in front of me. The projector coughed and clicked along behind me. And then, to top it off, Terry took my hand.

I tried to calm myself. I breathed deeply, holding the side of my slippery chair with my free hand and keeping myself rigid. Everything inside me screamed to take that chair and bend it over his head, but I managed to sit peaceably and keep my eyes on the screen. My mind screamed over and over, "How dare he touch me! How dare he want to?" I sat still, my hand in his, and I watched the show, and listened to the projector, and wanted to die.

When the movie ended, seemingly years later, we went outside and saw that it was starting to get dark. The clouds had thickened again, and lowered, shutting off any view for a mile or so. The air was colder than we had felt so far on the trip, well below freezing. We pulled our coats around us and walked down the street to the hotel and met the woman behind the counter.

She smiled as soon as she saw us.

"Good news," she said, no doubt realizing that bad news might mean an end to the continued success of her hotel. "We have a no-show. You can have the room now."

Terry filled out the paperwork and paid her, and I gathered my luggage. Before we left the lobby, though, I turned and smiled and thanked her. And I meant it. She had been kinder than I deserved, and I wanted to let her know that I appreciated it. Terry and I found our room and unloaded the luggage. It was small but comfortable and well kept. Before anything was unpacked, though, Terry turned on the television to look for a weather report. I didn't need to see one; I would not be flying again.

The news was the same all night: a storm was passing through from the south and would be clearing in the morning. Fair skies were forecast for the next afternoon and evening. Terry was encouraged. I was indifferent. The weather just didn't matter anymore. I had family in Brigham City, Utah, and family in southern California, and somebody, I was sure, would understand my situation and come help me home. If not, I would buy a bus ticket.

I hadn't returned Terry's warmness during the movie, and he seemed to understand that I didn't want to get any closer to him than I had to. We ate dinner at a cafe across the street and went back to the room. Terry turned on the television for the latest weather report. I called my mother again to let her know we wouldn't be home as expected. The kids were crying in the background. I heard one of them yelling, "mine, mine!" then another huge crash. I shuddered. My mother's voice was shaky.

"RaNelle," she said, "when are you coming home?"

"Right away, Mom. As soon as I can."

"RaNelle, they've ruined one of your father's paintings. They colored on it with their fluorescent markers and I can't get it off."

My heart sank. Over the years, my father had collected valuable oil paintings, some so beautiful that major magazines had come to photograph them for their covers. I could only imagine the cost of the damage.

"What did Dad do?" I ventured.

"He doesn't know yet. I can't bear to tell him." Her voice was getting weaker. "I just hid it. You'll have to tell him, RaNelle." I thought she might cry.

The weight of the world lay on my shoulders as I prepared for bed. I was twenty-five years old and I already felt fifty. The surge of adrenaline earlier had left me limp now, and I crawled under the covers in a kind of mental and emotional fog. I closed my eyes and envisioned snow and fog all around me; the tractor racing up at me; the little tree attacking our plane; the door popping open; ice cutting my skin; Terry yelling that we were going on, going on, going on; and Christina and Jason yelling mine, mine, mine. I imagined the crash of something big and important, and saw the painting smeared with fluorescent marker. I opened my eyes and saw the low, freshly painted Best Western ceiling, and I felt like crying.

I glanced at Terry in front of the TV and thought about our decision to divorce. It had resulted from a long history of problems in our marriage. Terry was the son of an alcoholic father and had learned to deal with problems by denying them, while I sometimes recklessly confronted issues head-on. We were opposites in many ways, and neither of us had the communication skills to bridge our differences. We married young and had experienced difficulties right from the start. In fact, four days after our wedding we had fought with each other and ended up driving around town looking for the courthouse to get divorce papers. We couldn't find it. Then we had decided to stay together for another few days to try and work things out. A few days had stretched into five years—and now I saw that things would never work out.

"Please, God, help me," I cried quietly. "I don't know what to do. I feel so lost, so confused. Please, please help me." I fell asleep to the sound of the voice on TV saying, "Well, folks, it's here. Looks like we could get our first snow tonight . . ."

Somehow Terry and I were in the plane again, and we were lost, snow and fog driving against the windshield, ice forming full-length crystals to block our view. We were blind to all but the mist and fog. The clouds broke suddenly, and the ground reared up at us, lifting to meet us, filling the windshield like a movie filling the screen, and I knew we were flying into a mountain. "Higher, higher, higher!" I yelled, begging Terry to pull the plane up, even though I knew the little craft could never make it. Then I was out of the plane, above it, watching with fascination as it hit the ground and skipped like a rock over trees and boulders. It struck the earth again, and jagged stones ripped through its belly, slicing into the cabin, tearing the plane apart. And as the red and white Beach Bonanza finally came to a stop, a huge fireball erupted from its fuel tank and filled the sky with dark, swirling smoke.

I knew I was dead.

I screamed and sat bolt upright in bed. I put my hands to my face. It was coated with sweat. Panic racked me. I knew the dream was a forecast of what would happen if I ever got in that plane again. But even more powerful than that was the feeling that the crash had already happened. That Terry and I had gotten into that plane and crashed against the side of a mountain, even though we knew better, even though it had been prophesied, and the terror of its seeming sureness gripped me like no fear had before. I must have awakened everybody in the hotel with my screaming—everybody but Terry. He just snored away. I grabbed him and shook him and pulled the covers back. Finally he turned over in a groggy daze and moaned, "What'sa matter?"

I grabbed his arm and said, "We're not getting in that plane tomorrow. I've had a terrible dream, and I know we'll crash if we do. I don't care what happens. I don't care how desperate you are to get home. I'm not flying tomorrow. Do you hear me?"

His eyes were still closed, and he settled his head a little deeper in the pillow.

"RaNelle," he said, "I had just planned on renting a car. We'll drive home and leave the plane here. Go back to sleep."

I was stunned. He had been listening to me. He had thought through the problem and had come up with a great solution. Of course. We'd just rent a car and drive home. It was a hundred times safer than flying, and we'd be home by evening. I *almost* wanted to hug him.

I lay back in bed, my mind still racing from the dream, seeing the plane glancing off the rocks, coming to a stop, and bursting into flames. Finally, fitfully, sleep overcame me.

I HAD BEEN HESITANT ABOUT FLYING SINCE I WAS A LITTLE girl. My father—who loved flying—was a pilot and took me up over southern California once. We were five thousand feet up, in a small plane, flying level alongside ten-thousand-foot mountains. Suddenly we plunged like a falcon out of the sky and I knew we were going to die. But my father was only playing with me. It was a strange form of entertainment. When he pulled us out of the dive, one of the mountains was so close it blazed by in a blur, and I thought we would hit it. I was only ten years old, but I swore I'd never fly again. There's nothing like a little plane against a big mountainside to get you to make resolutions.

Then I married a man who loved to fly. When Terry got his license shortly after we were married, I told him I wouldn't go up with him. He tried to persuade me by saying that we could make flying a family sport, but nothing short of unusual force—which he didn't employ—could get me to fly. So, when Terry came out of the bedroom one day holding an aviation magazine and calling out that he had found his plane, I couldn't believe it. I was stunned. I had figured he'd get his license, put in some hours on a rented plane, and get the bug out of him. But no, when Terry wanted something, he became passionate.

I read the ad. It said the plane was a 1946 V-tail Bonanza. This was 1984—the plane was nearly *forty* years old! Almost as old as Terry and me combined. I saw images of World War II movies and old beat-up planes with paint cracking off, windows shot out, and propellers falling off. I pictured Terry in goggles and a leather helmet. I said, "Terry, I don't think this is a good idea."

As usual, when I expressed an opposing viewpoint, he didn't seem to hear me. "I'm going to call now," he said. "We can go down to the airport today," and he headed for the phone.

Later that day in a cloverleaf hangar just outside Bakersfield, we saw the plane for the first time. When the gentleman selling the plane opened the hangar door, I couldn't believe what sat before us. It was the cutest, shiniest, red and white flying machine I could have imagined, and it was in immaculate condition with a shape much like newer planes I had seen. I thought these V-tail planes must be like Mercedes cars—tried and proven machines that simply don't need changing. This was not what I expected. I went up to it and laid my hand on the wing, and a sudden chill ran from the top of my head to my toes. I said, "Terry, don't buy this plane."

He stared at me. "Are you kidding? The price is perfect, and it's beautiful. Look at it."

"Terry, please. Don't buy it." Somehow I knew at that moment that this plane was a beautiful, immaculate death machine, that someday it would become our tomb. I said, "We're going to die in this plane."

"RaNelle, come on," he said. "You're exaggerating. It's just your fear of flying. Nothing's going to happen."

I knew this was not simply an irrational fear. There was something *to* this premonition. But when I saw the light in Terry's eyes, a light I'd never seen before, there was a moment of confusion, and the image of this plane as our tomb began to fade. Terry told me to get up in the cockpit and sit in the seat. There was only one cockpit door—it was on the passenger side. I hesitated a moment, then got into the plane. When I sat and ran my hand over the controls and looked out the window I felt a little more comfortable. But I would have to be convinced.

Terry climbed in over me and sat in the pilot's seat.

"Are you going to put the hours into this to make it worthwhile?" I asked.

"We'll fly it every weekend," he said. "We'll fly it constantly, and we'll put in the hours to become experts. It'll be good for us, RaNelle."

It was that thought that in the end made me relent. I put the premonition behind me and we bought the plane right there, using our entire life savings. It would be worth it, I thought, if it helped our marriage.

Our first trip together was not promising. We were climbing out of Bakersfield, heading west toward the Coast Range Mountains when suddenly the sound of the engine and propeller became a deafening roar. I turned to the right, where the roar was loudest, and saw the most beautiful, terrifying blue sky where the door should have been. I screamed and grabbed the left-side armrest in a clawlike grip. Terry looked over, saw the door flapping open, and said—or at least his lips seemed to say—"Close it." He had to be kidding; I wasn't budging. I yelled at him to land the plane, but he didn't seem to hear, so I screamed it again closer to his ear. He yelled, "No, just pull it shut!" I didn't seem to have any choice, so, still holding the armrest with my left hand, I reached out with my right arm, grabbed the handle and pulled. It wouldn't budge. The hinges were in front, like on a car door, and the wind streaming in behind it created a high-pressure system that would not allow it to close. I looked down and saw the patchwork of farms in western Kern County—directly below me. I quickly let go of the door and pulled back into the plane.

Terry yelled again, "Come on, RaNelle, close it!"

"No!" I screamed. "Land!"

"No! Close it."

This was quickly becoming one of the most open and direct discussions we'd ever had. Finally I reached out and tried to close the door again, but no matter how hard I pulled, it wouldn't close.

Terry got on the radio. "Bakersfield Tower, triple three niner victor," he said, identifying our plane. When the tower answered, Terry requested permission to turn back and land the plane. The tower gave permission, and he signed off. A few minutes later we were landing. The door shut without any problem once we were on the ground, and we turned the airplane around, taxiing back into the wind, and took off again.

Over the coming months we tried everything to fix that door. We put on new latches, old latches, metal fittings, solder, wood, glue, wax, cardboard, and finally decided to leave it alone and just remember to close it tightly before each take off. Periodically it would open in flight of its own accord, and we'd have to land again. Eventually we got to the point where we could just touch down, slow to about thirty-five miles per hour, shut the door, and take off again. Though inconvenient, it seemed an easy solution. But I never got used to it.

Terry had made his career in designing high-tech equipment for the oil and aerospace industries. He had always provided well for the family, but now he wanted to move. He had always wanted to live in Utah—a place with more space and fewer people—but I had been concerned about moving the family away from our roots. My worry was not over his ability to make a living in Utah—a large oil field lay just across the border in Wyoming—I was concerned about *my* ability to support the family alone if Terry and I couldn't work out our problems.

I had gone back to school to get my degree in communications and had been given an internship at a television station in Bakersfield. The internship was growing into an exciting and potentially rewarding position as a possible news producer. I wasn't interested in moving to another state if it meant jeopardizing my future and the livelihood of our two children. Terry and I had been to counseling already, and I wasn't naive enough to think that a move to another state, or to anywhere, would make our problems go away. We seemed locked into cycles of bitter bickering and stone silence that made the atmosphere at home intolerable. If Terry and I were going to split up, I wanted to be able to support myself.

When Terry mentioned to the counselor that he wanted to pursue a career in Utah, the counselor suggested that Terry and I make a trip together to see if a job and housing could be found. He said we should leave the children behind—that perhaps a week or two alone together would help us iron out a few things. Though I was dubious, I said I would go. In exploring my feelings I found that I did want to give our marriage one more chance. Maybe this trip was meant to be, and time alone together, planning a new beginning for our family in Utah, would draw us closer.

We made plans to fly our plane to Salt Lake City and rent a car for the drive up to Park City, where we would look for a new home.

Over the next few weeks I began to have a strange sense of foreboding about the trip. Something inside me warned me not to go. My stomach would knot whenever I thought about flying to Utah. I began having trouble sleeping and quickly found myself thinking the worst. I got two boxes and wrote Christina's name on one and Jason's on another. I started putting things in them that I wanted each child to have in case of my death.

One day while setting tables with a friend for a church luncheon, I told her about the trip, and a curious expression crossed her face.

"RaNelle," she said, "I don't want you to go."

"What do you mean?" I said. "Our plans are set. We've got hotel reservations and everything."

"I just have a bad feeling you won't be coming back." Her eyes filled with tears.

I assured her that I would be all right, but her words had rung clearly in my mind.

But despite what I felt before the trip, I continued with preparations. Terry also pushed the plans forward, and we became hopeful for a new beginning to our marriage. After all, a happy home was what our children needed most, and that was worth any sacrifice. My own desires overran the warning voice; I persuaded my mother to take the kids, and two days later we were on our way.

We flew toward Rialto, California, where my parents, Karl and Charlene Spoerl, lived. Blue sky and soft white clouds surrounded us as we left Bakersfield Airport. The children, sitting in back, seemed to enjoy the flight. Periodically we would fly into a cloud, the light around us dimmed and the cockpit cooled, and then we'd pop out and the light would dazzle us and make our skin tingle. The engine roared ahead of us, pulling us farther and farther away from the San Joaquin Valley with its orchards and open fields, and soon we

were facing the steep ridges of the Tehachapi Mountains—
wild, vertical peaks that when hidden by low clouds have
ended the careers of more than a few light-plane pilots. In
fact, these were the mountains where my father had teased me
by falling out of the sky like a bomb until I was sure we were
going to die. But today I was not afraid. We had clear sailing
above the Tehachapis, with cotton ball clouds like friends
around us and the grayish peaks like distant thoughts below.

Then, in a shock, I remembered a dream I'd had the night
before. I had been walking in a graveyard looking for a head-
stone. Finding it, I read my name on it and had woken up
terrified. Suddenly I knew that the dream applied to this trip.
I was going to die.

I looked out the window at the beautiful clouds sliding
peacefully past and heard the steady drone of the engine, but
my feelings were in turmoil. The dream's meaning came to
me with incredible power and a voice, almost audible, came
to my mind, saying: "Okay, RaNelle, make your decision.
How are you going to handle this?" I looked at my children.
Christina was coloring on a yellow legal tablet and Jason was
playing with a toy. I traded with Christina for a coloring
book, then got a pen and began writing on the tablet.

Terry looked over and saw:

LAST WILL AND TESTAMENT

"Ah, RaNelle," he said, "what are you writing?"

"What does it look like?"

"It looks like you're getting all worked up again." He
turned to face me. "What are you going to do, write out your
will right now?"

"That's right."

"Oh, come on, RaNelle . . ."

"No, think about it. What if we died on this trip? Who'd take care of everything?"

"Your mom would probably take the kids," he said. "They'd be all right."

"Maybe, but who takes everything else?"

"It all goes to the kids."

"Does it? You've got three thousand dollars in your pocket right now. What would happen to that?"

He stared at me. It was almost all the cash we had, and he knew the IRS—who had always paid unusual attention to him—would fall all over themselves getting it. Terry didn't say anything. He took the pad and made provisions for the money. Then I got the pad back and assigned rights and responsibilities for the house and other possessions, even our wedding rings, making sure that the children would be provided for as much as possible. But, we had no insurance; if we died, the children would get very little. I folded the pages and tucked them into Christina's suitcase. Moments later we landed in Rialto and I threw open the door and waved hello.

My parent's blue Cadillac was next to the runway. My brother, VaLoy, who was only eight, had come with them and had a camera in his hands. As soon as the kids saw Grandpa, Grandma, and Uncle VaLoy, they jumped out of the plane, and Christina went off to play with VaLoy, and Jason went walking with Grandpa. Terry got the kids' things out and began rearranging our luggage for balance, while Mom and I took the children's luggage to the car. I told her there were some papers in Christina's suitcase that she needed to look at when she got home.

"What are they?" she asked.

"Nothing, just some papers I want you to look at."

"What's in the papers?"

"Please, Mom, don't worry about it. It's nothing."

"RaNelle, what's going on?" She persisted. "Tell me."

I decided I didn't have any choice. She was going to know soon enough anyway. "I had a dream last night," I said, "and I was afraid it had something to do with this trip." I told her the dream and how it had come back to me in the plane. "Please," I said, "promise that if anything happens, you'll take the kids and love them the way I do. Promise me that."

My mother's eyes filled with emotion. "Of course, RaNelle. You know I will." Then she added, "I've raised seven of my own, you know."

At that moment I saw something wonderful in my mother. She'd given her life to raising her children, loving us, trying to make us happy. She had suffered her own difficulties and in spite of them had sacrificed greatly for us. My children would be in good hands.

Terry finished arranging the luggage and called me to come, but my mother said, "Please, RaNelle, don't go." It was the second time in two days I had heard this, but I couldn't stop now. With my children provided for, it seemed that my course was set and I was powerless to change it.

I climbed onto the wing. "RaNelle, don't go!" My mother followed me. She now had the yellow papers in her hand. I was sitting on the edge of the seat by the time she reached me. She was pale, and her knuckles were white from clutching the paper. "RaNelle . . ."

"Mom," I said, "just say a prayer that we'll be protected. Please. Let's leave it in the Lord's hands."

My father had reached us too, looking concerned, but saying nothing. He and Jason had found a wrecked plane behind the hangars. It had resembled our plane once but now looked like a large pop can smashed together for recycling. Seeing it, Dad also had felt an impression of foreboding, but wasn't sure if he should tell us. Months later, when I learned of this, I asked him, "Dad, why didn't you tell us? Why didn't you warn us?" I wanted to reach back in time and hear his warning and heed it. But then I saw the catch; the warning would have been given in vain. I had already been given enough warnings, but I wasn't listening; I had spent a week running from them.

Terry punched the ignition, but my mother would not step away.

"Mom," I called over the rising howl of the engine and propeller. "Stop worrying! Please, just take care of the kids." As the plane rolled forward, Christina and Jason broke free and ran after us.

"No," I yelled, half hanging out of the door. "Go back! Mom, grab the kids!" She ran forward and caught them before they reached us.

We gained speed and taxied to the end of the runway and turned around so we could take off into the wind. As we came back down the runway and passed them, I saw my mother still standing there holding Jason and Christina. She was close enough that I could see tears on her cheeks. Until that moment I didn't know how much my mother loved me.

Sunlight filled the cabin as we rose into the embrace of the warm sky. Everything glowed. Even the red wingtips sparkled in the brilliant sunlight. Inside, I suddenly felt calm and serene. Tranquility seemed to rest on me, but it was more expansive and pervasive than that; it seemed to fill the plane, distilling into every inch of the cabin. Even the engine seemed quiet—just a purring sound. Everything was behind us now—all the dread, all the fear, all the doubt. What lay ahead would take care of itself.

The trip into Salt Lake City was uneventful except for the magnificent display of fall colors on the sides of the Wasatch peaks. Once in Utah, a swath of brilliant colors along the mountains almost guided us to the city. The weather was absolutely perfect, the air crisp and light, almost sparkling. As we descended into the Salt Lake Airport I felt happier and more at peace than I had in months.

The next day we drove to Park City and rode through the neighborhoods to see if there were any homes for sale that we liked. As we got out on the road, I turned and saw the whole southern sky filling with hot-air balloons. The town was raising money for a boy who had been diagnosed with leukemia, and the balloons were part of a festival in his honor. This was a real town, I thought, the kind you read about in books, the kind that holds festivals for a sick child.

"Terry, I love this place," I said almost before I knew it.

"I know what you mean," he said. "I've loved it for years."

We found a new subdivision that appealed to us the moment we turned into it, and we got out of the rental car and walked down the sidewalks, watching the children play, studying the houses. On the second or third street, we saw a home for sale that was exactly what we were looking for, with a high-pitched roof to accommodate the winter snow, a large picture window, and a good-sized yard. It was perfect for a growing family. We went up to the door and knocked.

We couldn't really think of buying anything since Terry didn't have a job here, but walking through, we were charmed by the design of the rooms, and the floor plan was ideal. Before I knew it, Terry had made an offer and put a small cash deposit on it. Moments later we were outside.

"Terry, do you think that was wise?" I asked as we walked down the sidewalk.

"What do you mean—you like it don't you?"

"Yes, I love it, but I was just thinking, shouldn't we find a job first?"

"It'll come, RaNelle. We have to believe in ourselves. We're here to make a new beginning, right? This looks like the best place to start over that I've seen. In fact, it's not a bad place to end up."

It *was* a beautiful house, and we both loved the town. I only hoped finding a job would be as easy as finding the home.

We stayed in Salt Lake another week while Terry interviewed for various jobs. Then I noticed the weather growing colder. Yellow, orange, and red leaves began to fall, and I started growing impatient. We had been flying high, living a kind of fantasy, but I was feeling anxious to get back home, and I told Terry that I thought we should be leaving soon. But he hadn't made all the connections he wanted with the oil companies yet. "Let's just spend a couple more days here," he said. "Your folks aren't expecting us home yet, and as long as we're in Utah we ought to accomplish everything we came for."

The next day the weather turned chilly, and the following day, a cold rain began falling. My anxiety increased. We needed to get home. Later that day Terry dropped me off at a salon to get my hair permed, and I had time alone to think. I saw that Terry was serious about finding a job, just as he had been about buying the plane. He was leaving no stone unturned in his search. He knew what he wanted and there was no going back. We *would* be moving, I realized. And now, for the first time, I seriously thought about leaving my home in Bakersfield. I had friends there and family nearby. I also had my internship with the television station which offered real opportunities for growth. My colleagues were becoming successful and moving on, some to New York and others to Los Angeles. Who knew where I was headed? I had been told that with my talent and work habits I could go far. The producers seemed to like me. And in a medium where looks can be the deciding factor between talented people, my blond hair and blue eyes gave me an edge. I was very objective about this. I knew that the same attributes that made strange men want to buy me dinners in restaurants or hold doors open for me were the same ones that could put me over the top in television. Like one of the producers said after a show: "RaNelle, you've got what it takes. Stay with it."

Was I going to stay with it, or was I coming to Utah to begin at the bottom again at a Salt Lake station? Was I going to leave everything I had known in California and start over in this strange, beautiful land? Did I want my children raised here? They were too young to know the difference between life in California and life in the mountains, but one day they would. Is this the life I wanted for them—a little slower, a lot more rustic?

And finally, what about Terry? Did I want to stay with him? We were having a fairy-tale vacation in the Rocky Mountains, but it had been like ten carefree days spent with a good friend—not with a husband. It was not like a second honeymoon with the man I loved, not like the beginning of something new and wonderful. What did this mean?

When my hair was done I had more questions than answers.

Terry saw my perm as I got in the car and asked how much it cost. Within a couple of stoplights we were in another argument. But the rain that had started earlier was falling harder now, with lightning striking around us, and we quickly became more concerned with the weather and possible flying conditions than we were with my perm. We got back to the room and Terry called the weather service to see if the storm would let up soon. When he hung up, he said, "The storm's supposed to pass through tonight, but there's another one coming in from the south tomorrow."

"When can we leave?" I asked.

"The ceiling of the new storm is about eight or nine thousand feet—plenty of room to fly in. But they said if we leave tomorrow when this storm breaks up, we'll make it to Las Vegas before the new storm comes in."

"But if it's coming from the south, we'll be flying right into it."

"We'll be okay. We just have to leave when this storm is heading out. I guess they know what they're talking about."

"Terry, I don't have a good feeling about this."

"Why doesn't that surprise me? You wanted to leave today if I remember right."

"We should have left yesterday."

He threw his suitcase on the bed. "Better get packing, RaNelle. We're out of here first thing in the morning."

We packed and spent the rest of the day in silence. A knot was growing in my stomach that couldn't be ignored. We were headed for disaster—our marriage, the move here, our flight tomorrow. Something, everything, was wrong. By that evening a quiet, but terrible understanding was beginning to grow.

Terry and I went to dinner and again not much was said. Everything was finally ready for the trip; all we had to do was wait for the storm to clear.

Back at the hotel, Terry went to the front desk to see if the indoor pool was still open. I walked over to the elevator and saw my reflection in the mirrors next to the elevator. Despite the rain, I was pleased to see that the perm was holding, and I noticed how long my hair was, past my shoulders. I brought my hand up and touched my face. I looked nice, I thought, maybe even beautiful. But as I took a moment to reflect, I noticed a strange coldness surrounding me. I saw an emptiness where once feeling and happiness had been. My face and hair looked nice, but my heart was frozen. It was beating, and blood coursed through it, but I felt no emotion, no life, no purpose for being there. The quiet understanding that had begun earlier continued. I looked at myself in the mirror and thought about Terry. "Is life with him what you really want?" I asked. "Do you love him?" I thought of the past five years and the prospect for more of the same. "Can you be happy giving the rest of your life to him?" And looking into my own eyes I knew the answer to each of these questions. Quietly and clearly the answers came: no, no, no.

Terry came back, and we stood silently waiting for the elevator to come down. It opened, and we got in. The interior was lined with mirrors, and I saw myself again. And I saw Terry.

"It's over isn't it?" I said.

He thought for a moment, and I watched his face. He never looked at me. "Yeah, I guess so."

"I just don't feel anything anymore," I said softly.

"Neither do I."

I watched him in the mirror and felt no love or compassion. A deadness replaced all feeling. I didn't even feel a loss. The doors opened and we went to our room. I stood near the bed and saw myself again in the mirror above the dresser.

"Do you want to file, or do you want me to file?" I asked.

He didn't answer as he stood on the other side of the bed. He quietly studied the maps in his hands, and I continued to gaze in the mirror. I don't remember if he ever answered my question. I don't remember if I ever asked it again. Things would take care of themselves. I had to get home now and take care of the kids and find my life—find myself. Would I become an acclaimed news reporter, or a single mother on welfare? Would I finish school, or would I give up? I was about to find out who and what I was for the first time ever, and I suddenly felt a spark of emotion, of energy and excitement that had been gone until then. The ten days in Salt Lake and Park City were meaningless now. Life had let me bail out for a week and a half. But now, on this rainy, dreary night, life was coming back with a vengeance, taking me by storm, and for the first time in months—maybe years—I couldn't wait to jump into it with all the gusto and fight I had. I was ready to battle it blow for blow.

I couldn't wait to get home.

WOKE UP IN DELTA, THE DREAM OF OUR PLANE TEARING
through rocks and trees on a mountainside still with me. I
lay in the hotel bed and reflected on the disastrous trip of the
day before, the fearful flight from Salt Lake City, the emergency landing, the farmer, the movie, the oath that I had made
with God that I would not get back in that plane. I remembered Terry's solution and knew exactly what to do. I opened
the drawer in the nightstand and looked for a phone book. I
found a Gideon Bible, a Book of Mormon, a pad of stationary,
a little pamphlet about the town of Delta—everything but a
phone book. I rummaged through the drawer again, my concern growing. "I can't believe it," I said aloud, knowing full
well that Terry was asleep. "There's no phone book here." I
grabbed the pamphlet about Delta to see if a car rental agency
had advertised there. To my amazement, the ten-page pamphlet *was* the phone book—not only for Delta, but for the
whole county. I went to the Yellow Page. No luck.

"There's no car rentals," I said flatly. "Nothing at all." I felt
a numbness coming over me.

Terry stirred in bed.

"What?" he said.

"What do we do, Terry? There are no car rentals in Delta."

He rolled over and rubbed his eyes, still not awake.

I turned to "Farming Equipment." My mind was racing. If we couldn't get a car, we'd get a truck, or a tractor, and go as fast as we could to somewhere with a rental car. I found a number for farm rentals in Delta and called it.

"Hello," came the raspy voice. I had forgotten how early it was. For all I knew, this was somebody's home and I had just woken him. "Do you rent trucks?" I asked.

"Trucks?"

"Yes, trucks."

"What kind of trucks?"

"I don't care. Any kind. We just need to get to Fillmore. Do you rent trucks to Fillmore?"

"Nope," he said. "All's we got is farm equipment."

"Well, how about renting us a tractor? It's only thirty miles or so to Fillmore. We'll leave it there and get a car."

He paused a long moment. "Ma'am," he said, "all's we got is combines and harvesters—things like that—and we don't rent one way."

We said good-bye and hung up, but I actually would have done it. I would have ridden an alfalfa cutter, taking up the whole road, if it would have gotten us closer to a rental car.

Terry had gotten out of bed and was at the TV again looking for a weather report.

"Nothing," I said, putting down the phone. "We can't even rent a tractor."

"I can't find anything about the weather," Terry complained. "Could you look out the window and see what it looks like?"

I reached over and pulled back the curtains and was shocked by the change. Everything was white.

"Snow!" I yelled.

Terry looked at me from the foot of the bed. "What? How much?"

Being from southern California I had no idea how to measure snow without sticking something in it. All I knew was that it looked like a lot. "It snowed three feet," I said. "There's three feet of snow out there."

"What?" He came to the window. "Nah, there's only three or four inches on the cars," he said studying the roofs of the cars in the parking lot. "I've got an idea. Come sit down." He went back to the bed and sat on the foot of it.

"I'm not getting in that plane," I said, staying by the window.

"No, listen, I've got an idea."

It was one of Terry's ideas that had gotten us into this predicament, and I wasn't interested in hearing any more of them. But, on the other hand, I didn't have any ideas of my own. And I was desperate to get home, both to rescue my mother and to start my own life again. "I'm not getting in the plane, Terry."

"No, listen, look at this." Terry had the airport log that listed airports and their services. "Look, they have rental cars in Fillmore. All we have to do is get there and we can drive home. No problem."

"I know that, Terry. What do you think I've been trying to do?"

"So, what we'll do is this: we'll take off and fly to Fillmore, rent a car, and drive home. It's only fifteen minutes—tops—to Fillmore."

"Terry, please, I don't want to go up again. I mean it."

"But we've got to get home, RaNelle. We can't stay here."

"Why not?"

"I checked with the desk last night. The motel is booked solid with workers building a new power plant outside of town. There are no rooms tonight." He looked me in the eye and repeated: "We've got to get home, RaNelle."

I'll never forget the numbness that came over me at that instant. When Terry repeated "We've got to get home," we both knew just how desperately we wanted it. In my numbness I became deaf to that voice within urging me to stay in Delta, to do anything but fly. I only saw the prospect of a fifteen-minute flight and the relief of getting in a car and driving home as fast as we could. We gathered our things in silence—if Terry was talking I didn't know it—and went to the front desk to check out.

The same lady was on duty. I felt sorry for her, realizing that she must have worked all night. A concerned look came over her face as she saw us with our luggage.

"Are you going to fly this morning?" she asked.

"We're going to give it a try," Terry said.

The woman looked stunned. "You're really flying back to California today?"

"No," said Terry, "just to Fillmore to rent a car."

Her voice was stronger when she spoke again. "No. I don't want you flying this morning."

I was surprised by her sudden tone. "Why not?" I asked. "Why don't you want us flying?"

"I don't know. I just have a funny feeling about it."

A chill went up my back. I'd had that same feeling only hours before.

"It's just," she continued hesitatingly, "I just don't feel you should."

Terry shrugged. "We have to go," he said. "We can't stay here another night. You're booked."

"Yes, but. . ." She thought a moment. "Look, why don't you take my car to Fillmore. I can get someone to drive it back later." She pointed to her old, green Chevy parked just outside the door.

I was surprised by the offer and the thought went through my mind, ungenerously, that even in her car we might not make it. I was uncomfortable with so much charity, however, from someone I didn't really know. Actually, I was uncomfortable with charity from anybody.

"No, no," I said, "we couldn't put you out like that. It's only, what, twenty-seven miles. We'll be all right."

Some moments are etched indelibly in a person's mind. This one is etched in mine—her tender, pleading look of concern, her eyes suddenly filling with tears. Her words again, "Please don't go. Let me help you."

I see myself, standing there, shaking my head, saying, "No, thank you."

Terry was getting anxious. "It's really not a big deal," he said. "It's just fifteen minutes. What can happen in fifteen minutes? Look how long we've been standing here. Fifteen minutes is nothing."

Those words, too, have echoed in my mind.

Terry had told me many times that I had to conquer my fears. Deep down, I suspected he was right, at least partially. Sometimes my fears were justified, as are many fears people have, but there had been times, I was certain, when my fears were unsupported by circumstances.

"We'll be okay," I said to her. "Don't worry about us."

"Are you sure?" she asked, her voice still pleading.

"Sure," Terry said, "we'll be fine."

"Well, at least let me drive you to the airport. Will you let me do that for you?"

Since Delta didn't have a taxi service, we didn't have much choice. She put a sign on the counter saying she'd be back soon, and we picked up our luggage and stepped outside to the car. The bite of the cold was the first thing I noticed.

Clouds of frozen vapor hung in the air from each breath, lingering in the same place long after we had walked away. Heavy, wet snow gushed from under our shoes with each step. I had worn a pair of clear plastic jelly shoes, currently in fashion in California but inadequate in four inches of snow, and my feet got soaked.

We put our stuff in the trunk, then after banging slush off our shoes and pulling our coats tighter around us, we got in the car. I was wearing a turtleneck, an angora sweater, my ski coat, and a pair of Levis. Terry had on a pair of Levis, shirt, sweater, and jacket.

I looked out the window. The sky had been painted granite gray, the clouds unbroken and as foreboding as anything we flew through yesterday. We would just have to fly under them, I told myself firmly. Staying below the clouds, we would be all right.

The Chevy's frozen engine was delinquent in answering, but finally turned over, and we pulled out of the parking lot and drove slowly through the slush on the two-lane road. The car slid once or twice on slow turns but, ten minutes later, we managed to arrive at the airport without incident. She made us promise to call her as soon as we landed in Fillmore. I wrote her number on a piece of paper and put it in a bag where I'd be sure to see it. We thanked her, and she wished us luck, asking us once more to take her car. We said, thank you, but no, and she drove away. I will never forget her—an angel at a moment we needed one, and wiser than we knew.

Terry threw the luggage into the plane and asked me to arrange it while he cleared the snow from the wings. Without gloves though, his hands were soon red and cramped with cold. He cleared the tops of the wings first, then the tips, and finally everything else he could reach on the plane. When he was done I got out and stood on the wing so he could get through the door, then I climbed in and banged the door shut. Just to be sure, I opened it and banged it again. It's still an FAA rule to shout "Clear" out the window and then "Propeller noise" before the propeller turns over. Of course, nobody was within two miles, but Terry did it anyway and started the engine. We went through the safety check with me calling out the list and Terry working the controls. The flaps, rudders, and ailerons were fine, for the time being. Ice could build up in just a few seconds in the air. The oil was full and clean. We checked for water in the gas tank. There was none, and we had plenty of fuel. Terry called out "3339V" on the radio to warn any approaching aircraft of our take off, then accelerated down the runway. It was nine o'clock, and I was just beginning to feel the first twinges of hunger, but we could worry about that in Fillmore.

The drag on the plane was terrific. The wet snow on the runway held us back more than we anticipated, and now we noticed that ice was forming on the wing tips again. It wasn't much, because Terry had dried them with a cloth at the last second, but the drag was magnified that much more. Terry pulled up on the yoke, but we weren't getting any lift. He pulled a little tighter, but we seemed glued to the ground, chugging through the slush and snow. I saw a wire fence rushing at us from the end of the runway, and I felt the first real surge of danger. What we were doing was becoming terribly clear.

"Terry! Stop, stop, stop!"

"It's too late. I can't . . . We can make it!"

"No, Terry, please stop. Now!"

"Hang on, RaNelle. We'll make it."

The runway ended and we hit gravel. The fence was only a few yards away when the wheels left the ground. The fence skimmed beneath us, and, incredibly, the landing gear stayed with the plane instead of with the fence. But now the plane was struggling. A Beach Bonanza is one of the most powerful single-engine aircraft you can get, capable of going well over two hundred miles per hour, and when it leaves the ground it usually pops off the pavement and throws you against the seat as it charges upward. But now the plane flew like it was churning through water.

"Turn around, Terry!" I yelled. "Turn around! I knew this would happen, I knew it. I've got that feeling again, Terry. I've got that terrible feeling. We've got to turn back!"

"We'll stall if we turn. We're too low."

But I could see that we were beginning to rise. "Turn this thing around, now! Don't you understand? Something bad is going to happen. Something terrible! Turn around!" In my mind I heard the haunting reverberations of Terry's simple question: *What can happen in fifteen minutes?*

I was screaming now. "Please, Terry, go back! Go back!" But Terry fended off my screams with logic.

"Calm down, RaNelle. Everything's okay now. Look out the window and enjoy the scenery. Look," he said, pointing directly ahead, "there's Fillmore. Just off the nose."

To my amazement Fillmore lay before us like a little plastic model, a toy town snuggled against mountains nine or ten thousand feet high. The Wasatch Front dwarfed the little town, the peaks disappearing into the frozen, gray mass of clouds. But suddenly everything seemed okay. I couldn't believe that I had panicked. Fillmore was just a few minutes away, lying serenely below the same ceiling that we were skimming under. Everything *was* okay, just like he had said.

All we had to do now was find the airport, which was near a mushroom factory. It was almost impossible to miss from the air; the buildings and greenhouses had a unique configuration. But as we began to come into Fillmore airspace, the cloud level quickly dropped. Terry nudged the yoke down as we skimmed through the first wisps of gray mist. We came out of them for a moment then hit clouds again, and he nudged the yoke lower.

"Look," he said, pointing right of the nose, "there's the mushroom factory." I looked down and spotted it, but I couldn't see the airport.

"Where's the airport, Terry?"

"Right by the mushroom factory, remember?"

"I know, but I can't see it? Can you?"

He was silent as he scanned the ground. We went through clouds again, and he took the plane lower. We were only a couple hundred feet off the ground. I realized my hands were clenching the armrests, and I tried to relax. We went right over the factory, and Terry asked me to try again to find the airport. We both knew where it was supposed to be; we'd flown over it before. But now it was hidden under a shroud of slush and snow, and the little metal building that served as the tower blended in with surrounding farm buildings. Knowing that Fillmore's airport was manned, we turned the radio on and began calling. No answer. We were right over them, and either they couldn't hear us or the airport was deserted. We called again and again, trying to find somebody to help us, but we were answered only by static.

Like a sheet lowering onto a bed, the clouds dropped suddenly to the ground. I had never seen anything like it. In moments we were enveloped in fog and swirling, blinding snow. Terry lowered the plane again as low as he dared, almost skimming housetops, and we could only faintly see ground.

"There's no airport there," I said to him as we passed over the mushroom factory again. "Terry, we're in trouble."

"I'm going to call Cedar City," he said. In moments a controller responded, but the transmission was so cluttered with static that we couldn't make it out. Next, we tried Salt Lake but got only static. Delta's airport was unmanned, as we had found out yesterday, so we had nowhere to land and nowhere to turn for help.

What can happen in fifteen minutes?

I was afraid we were flying too close to the ground and I said, "Terry, pull up and head back to Delta. The ground is lower there, maybe the airport will be under the clouds."

"Okay," he said. "I'm going to make one more slow turn."

"Terry, look out!" A juniper bush flew by at eye level. "The ground!"

Terry pulled to the left, yanking back on the yoke and we were thrust against our seats as the plane took off like a rocket. I screamed louder and harder than I ever had, completely losing control. I was hysterical, not knowing or caring that I had just wet my pants. The windows were enshrouded in fog again. We had no idea where the mountainside was that we had just missed.

"We're not going to make it!" I screamed. "We're not going to make it! We're going to crash!"

"Shut up!" Terry yelled, "I can't fly." His knuckles were white on the yoke. "Let me fly!"

But I continued to scream uncontrollably, not realizing that I had stopped breathing and my face was turning purple. "RaNelle!" he said. "Breathe! Stop screaming." He suddenly hit me on the chest. "Breathe!" he commanded.

The blow stopped my screaming, and I tried to calm down and breathe again. I forced myself to inhale, then exhale, inhale, then exhale. I was shaking so hard I would have fallen off the seat if not for the seat belt. My body was charged with adrenaline.

"Now listen to me," he said. "We're going to circle down and make an emergency landing. Let me know if you see anything." He pushed the yoke down again and took us lower.

I began to pray. "Please, God, if you get me through this, I swear—I swear I'll do anything. I know what I said yesterday, but I'll do anything this time. I'll give all my money to the church. I'll never spank my kids again. I'll never cuss again." I went on and on. Then my mind seemed to clear somewhat, and I said over and over: "Let angels be on our wing tips. Let angels be on our wing tips. Please, Heavenly Father, let angels lift our wings and guide us down." I strained to see the ground, trees—anything—but all I saw was snow and fog. We went lower, and Terry said to let him know if I felt the wheels hit ground. Suddenly the clouds broke and we saw a wide road fifty or sixty feet below us. Several cars were on it. The road seemed even more welcome than the airstrip we had seen yesterday in Delta. But what road was this? Then it hit me—this was Interstate 15, the main highway between Salt Lake City and Las Vegas. Clouds smothered us again, preventing our view, but I knew what Terry had in mind.

"We're going to land," he said, dipping the plane a few feet lower.

I didn't complain. Interstate 15 seemed like an absolutely perfect place to land right then. We were still in the clouds, and Terry dipped the plane again. We hoped the road continued straight, not turning, leaving us flying over desert, or worse, into a mountain.

"Let me know when the wheels hit," he yelled, and we popped below the blinding snow and saw that we were about to land on top of a moving semi truck. It was just ahead of us, but we were gaining on it in a perfect approach for landing. Cars were lined up in front and behind it.

"No! No! No!" I screamed, and Terry pulled the yoke up and shot us into the clouds again. The driver of the semi probably never saw us, but he must have heard us. We were back up in the blinding snow and icy mist again, and I was beginning to feel sick to my stomach. Terry made another turn trying to stay near the freeway, and I thought I would throw up.

"Grab the maps!" Terry yelled. "See where we are."

I fought my nausea, found the map for the Fillmore area and opened it. I knew we had just passed eastward over Interstate 15, so I checked our instruments and looked back at the map.

"Oh my gosh, Terry! Turn back! The mountains come down to the freeway here. The mountains! Turn back! Turn back!" I almost grabbed the yoke from him.

"No, wait," Terry shouted. "I just saw a dirt road." I could see nothing but gray; the clouds covered us like a shroud. We must have been flying right over Fillmore, but we couldn't see a thing. The mountains were here too—somewhere. Perhaps within yards, or feet.

I was getting dizzy. I thought it was fear that caused it, or all the bouncing around, but soon I realized that it was vertigo. In the clouds, with snow racing past us, our turning one way and then another, I had lost my sense of direction. I couldn't tell if we were flying upside down or sideways, if we were ascending or descending, going forwards, or even backwards. Time and motion seemed to stop, and I existed in a stationary position while the world swirled around me. The instruments said that Terry had gone directly east, probably over the town, and had just banked thirty degrees to the south. The map had indicated mountains in that direction too. But my sense of direction and equilibrium were lost. I had no idea where we were, or even if we were moving.

"Find the road!" Terry yelled. "RaNelle, look for the road!" He lowered the plane again and slowed to 125 miles per hour.

I looked out the windshield and saw ground directly in front of us. At first I wasn't sure it was there, then it filled the whole window.

"The ground is coming! The ground is coming!" I yelled. I had the strangest feeling that we were standing still and the ground was rushing at us. I looked at the horizon on our instrument panel and became more confused. We were flying level. Why was the ground coming up at us? It was just like in my dream.

"It's a mountain, Terry!"

Before I got the words out of my mouth our propeller chopped through a juniper tree, and it seemed I could hear every sickening chop of the blades. Terry pulled all the way back on the yoke and tried to fly up the mountain, but our speed after hitting the tree was too slow, and the ground was rushing up fast. Quickly we were surrounded by tall boulders, and we slammed into the earth, belly first. We glanced off the ground like a rock skipping on water and slammed into the earth again. For a moment I actually felt exhilarated as the G-forces threw us forward and then up, twisting us from side to side. I just relaxed and felt the thrill of the best amusement park ride imaginable. We skipped off the tops of boulders and ricocheted off the sides of others. I saw sparks flying off the wings as they ground against granite slabs. Then I saw a small outcropping of rocks ahead of us, only three or four feet tall, and I knew the plane, which was beginning to nose into the earth, would hit it head-on, and we would die. In that moment I said, "Heavenly Father, please forgive me for everything I've done. Take care of my kids. Please, take care of my kids."

Jagged rocks knifed up through the belly of the plane, tearing away the cabin floor. I threw my feet up on the dash and watched the floor disappear beneath me as one boulder after another shot through the cabin. I looked out the windshield and watched the wall of rocks growing in size. Then I was thrown against the side of my seat as the plane suddenly spun to the right and nosed deeper into the ground. We came to a stop, our nose and left side almost touching the rock wall. Immense relief flooded over me, and I was surprised that I was still alive.

Silence enveloped us.

I quickly turned to Terry and saw that he was okay. "Oh, my gosh," I said, "we just survived a plane crash."

Terry was silent a moment, as if in a daze, then began tearing at his seat belt. "Get out! Get out!" he screamed.

I couldn't figure out what he was doing. Why was he so frantic? "What's the matter with you?" I said. Then I saw yellow and blue flames curling over the windshield on his side. They were coming up from the bottom of the fuselage and were already engulfing his side of the plane. I knew I had to get out, not just for me, but because the only door was on my side. Terry was trapped. Suddenly I smelled gasoline fumes in the plane and felt intense heat coming up from where the floor should have been. I knew that aviation gasoline had an octane of 105 and was one of the most flammable compounds on earth. The fuel line going underneath the cabin had been ripped open and was spilling gasoline all over the rocks and part of the floor. The fumes were almost overwhelming. In turning to get out, I glanced down where the heat was strongest and saw my jelly shoes melt off my feet in less than a second. Then I felt an incredible pain on my right thigh and saw that paint had melted off the ceiling and had dripped onto my jeans, burning into my flesh, sizzling into me like melted butter. Two more globs of paint landed on my thigh, and I frantically undid my seat belt, grabbed the door handle, and yanked. Nothing happened. I tried to force it, but it wouldn't open. The door that always popped open when it wasn't supposed to was jammed shut. Terry screamed, pleading, for me to get out, and I spun around, lifted my legs, and kicked at the door.

Metal screamed as the door flew open, and it felt like somebody put a blow torch on my face. I heard a tremendous "whoosh," felt incredible heat, and then I was blown out of the plane onto the wing. Firefighters call it backdraft. When the door opened, fresh oxygen surged into the cabin, mixing with the fumes and igniting instantaneously. The flames scoured my face and upper body, and when the fumes exploded I was thrown out onto the wing. I landed on my feet and stood for a moment before realizing I was on fire.

Flames leapt from my cheeks and chin. I brought up my hands and tried to beat them out, but my hands were on fire too. All of me was on fire. I fell to my knees, the pain so intense that I had almost no strength. But the sight of the flames coming up from my face horrified me, and I tried to beat them out again. Raising my hands this time I could see the skin of both hands hanging loose. The skin had melted off and was hanging down like inside-out surgical gloves from my fingertips. They hung down seven or eight inches, and I could even see fingerprints on the ghostly gloves. I tried to crawl, and the thought occurred to me that I was like a stuntman on fire, and I thought, what does a stuntman do? He drops and rolls to get the flames out, but there was nowhere for me to roll. I saw only jagged rocks and boulders around me.

Then I saw a slushy area of snow between two rocks, so I crawled down what was left of the wing and fell into the snow. I got to my hands and knees, and began to pack the snow onto my hands because they hurt the most. But the melted skin hanging from my hands got in the way. The weight of the gloves made my hands feel like all of my nails were being ripped off my fingers, and in a surge of desperation to rid myself of the pain, I grabbed the skin from my right hand and yanked it off. Pain exploded from my hand. A white, jelly-like tissue was exposed where the skin had been. I grabbed the skin from the other hand and ripped it off too, and my body buckled from the sudden agony.

Flames were crawling up my face, eating into my lips and nose and cheeks. Flames whipped against my eyes and I tried to take off my coat to cover my face. But it was on fire too—large chunks of it were falling on my pants and starting fires on my legs. Frantically I tried to smother the flames again, starting with my face, but I felt myself weakening, the fumes of my burning skin horrifying me, the pain filling me, terrifying me, eating me alive, and I knew I would die. I fell to a sitting position, a human inferno.

Snow hit my face. Then my hands. Snow pelted me on the head and soaked my arms. I looked up and was amazed to see slush and snow falling all around me. A sudden wind was whipping snow hard against me, and in an instant the flames were out. Then, just as suddenly, the squall stopped and the air was calm. I heard the flames of the plane still crackling, but the importance of this didn't register.

I knew the flames on my body were out, but I didn't know how badly I was hurt. I looked cross-eyed at my nose and saw only something like black ash. I put my fingers to it, and ash fell away, removing part of my nose. I ran my tongue over my lips, and they fell away in charred clumps of ash, completely exposing my teeth. When my lips fell off I thought numbly, "Uh oh, my lips fell off. I shouldn't have tried to lick them." I used my fingers to feel my chin, and I could tell that it was gone, leaving only an indentation where the cartilage had been burned away. I touched my head and found that my hair was gone, except for a little mat of singed roots. The middle of my forehead had no skin, and I could feel the raw bone piercing through the skin on my temples. Smoke rose all around me, smoke from my body—what remained of my body—and I smelled the sickening-sweet odor of burnt flesh. Nausea overcame me, and my stomach retched.

Searing, crippling pain rose from my thighs, and I thought I might pass out again. I forced my hands to peel back what was left of my jeans, which were mostly burned away in front. In a fog of pain I tried to put my fingers under the material covering my left thigh, only to realize that it wasn't denim that covered my leg; it was the charred flesh from another burn. Fresh pain rose from my left foot, which was pinned under me, and I wondered if I had broken it. Gently using my hands to guide my leg, I brought it out in front of me and saw that both the shoe and sock had burned off. Severe burns on the top of my foot and ankle exposed the bones. I didn't know if I would be able to walk. I tried to get up, but was too weak and sat back down.

Something was stuck to my chest. I peered down and found a piece of carpet glued there, about three feet long and sticking out by a foot on both sides. The carpet, which had once covered the dash of the cockpit, had been blown out of the plane with me and had somehow affixed itself to my chest.

It covered me from my collarbone to my waist. I gently tried to remove it, fighting through the pain in my hands and fingers, but the carpet wouldn't budge; its backing was melted to my skin.

Another wave of nausea and weakness swept over me, and I realized that I was in serious danger. I had survived the fire, but my body wasn't functioning right. Pain racked every fiber of me, but I couldn't stand up, couldn't cover myself, couldn't think. And I knew, deep within, that I was dying. Weakness buckled me, and for a moment I considered letting it overtake me altogether, to smother me, until pain and consciousness were erased. Until life, gratefully, departed. But something inside me rebelled. Something was fighting for life. A sudden thought shook me to the core.

Where was Terry?

He had made it out, hadn't he? But where had he gone—to get help? No. Terry wouldn't leave me like this. I was on my feet, all other thoughts cancelled; sudden strength filled me, and I grabbed the broken wing to pull myself back up to see. As I forced myself through the pain in my hands and crawled onto the wing, I was amazed to see twenty-foot flames soaring into the sky above the body of the plane. The heat drove me back. The entire cockpit was a huge, white-hot candle, and in the middle of that candle Terry's body lay slumped over the yoke. I knew with a sickening understanding that he was burning alive. The flames shot up around him like a waterfall in reverse, completely engulfing him. The roof was gone now, leaving only stark metal ribs, caging Terry and the yoke in a bleak skeleton of fire. I lunged toward the plane to pull him out, but again the heat drove me back. I yelled with all my might: "Terry, get out! Get out!"

There was no movement.

"Get out! Get out!" I was crying. I was screaming. "Get out! Get out! Get out!" The flames roared all around him, above him, on him, but he didn't move. I couldn't see whether he was still locked in his seat belt or not. All I could tell was that he was engulfed in flames. And the sight sickened me.

My husband was burning alive, suffering as he lay locked in the flames. "No, Terry, no," I cried. "Please don't feel it." And then, "Please, God, let him go quickly." As the heat consumed the plane around him, the emptiness of despair washed over me. He was dying, or dead now, and I was alone. Incredibly, it wasn't until this moment that I realized how much I needed Terry—how much I loved him. After all we had been through, despite all the anger and heartache and pain, Terry and I had tried to love each other—because somehow, we truly needed each other.

But now it was too late.

I turned my back to the flames and felt anger rising in me.

"God, this isn't fair!" I shouted up into the gray sky. "How dare you leave me alone to die like this! We've worked hard to be what you wanted. We've tried to be the best people we could be. And now you let Terry die, and you abandon me, leaving me to suffer and die on this mountain. How dare you abandon me!" I looked up into the heavy mist and felt my whole body shaking. "If there's a God alive, I need your help! Do you hear me? If there's a God alive, I need your help, and I need it now!"

Then, as if the heat which was all around me had only now touched me, I felt the shame of what I had just done. The guilt of my presumption and anger made me cringe. But then the most amazing peace came over me, and I got off the wing and sat on the rock near the puddle of slush. Peace continued to fill me, to direct me, and I bowed my head. For the first time, perhaps in my life, I prayed with all my heart.

"Dear Heavenly Father, please help me. Please help Terry if you can. Please forgive me for yelling at you. Please, Father, help us."

I had no lips. My tongue was already swelling in my mouth, but I uttered this prayer in clarity and utter humility. I felt it rise from the depths of my soul, and I knew that God heard me. For a moment I felt as if he were right beside me.

I stood up, the idea occurring to me that perhaps somebody had heard the crash and was coming at this very moment to find us. Cupping my hands as best I could to my mouth, I began yelling for help. Over and over I cried into the fog. The heat was still intense behind me, and I noticed that the snow and slush that had fallen only minutes before was evaporated around the plane now.

Smoke still rose from my body, choking me as I inhaled to yell.

But the peace lent me a confidence that I hadn't felt until then. I knew that somebody was going to help us. I had a certainty. God had not abandoned us. We would not be alone much longer.

I caught a movement out of the corner of my eye and looked back at the plane. The movement came again. In the cockpit Terry's right hand was going up. He was raising his right arm, and I could tell that it wasn't caused by the heat contracting his muscles. He was alive. I knew by the peace within me that he was completely and wonderfully alive. When his arm was almost extended, he stood up in the flames, his head and shoulders protruding through where the ceiling had been. He stood still for a moment, then with his right arm still extended, he stepped away from his seat and through the flames of the inferno. He came out seemingly unharmed onto the wing. Then he lowered his hand and continued toward me. I was dumbfounded.

A moment later he stood next to me.

"Where's the man that helped me out?" Terry asked. "Did you see him?"

I stared at him. His face and hands were red, as if he had a sunburn, but other than that he looked fine. He appeared unscathed, except for the redness.

"What man, Terry? I didn't see any man." My heart was racing. Metal had melted all around him. The cockpit was consumed. How did he survive? Even his clothes were intact, no singe marks. I could see, looking more closely, that his hands were burned more severely than I had thought, but everything else was impossibly untouched. He continued to study me, standing like a statue.

"The Lord heard your prayer, RaNelle," he said. "He meant for us to be together. We need each other."

I was astonished by these words. Where had they come from? How did he know this? And I realized that what had just happened would amaze me, thrill me, and at times confuse me for the rest of my life. The miracle wasn't just that he had survived; the greater miracle was what he had learned.

It was the same thing I had learned just a moment ago while sitting on the rock.

We needed each other—whether we wanted each other or not.

Terry and I looked at each other for what seemed a long time, then his gaze shifted, almost as if he were coming to himself, and he said, "RaNelle, what do we do?" His look was different, more pleading, more fearful.

"I don't know," I mumbled through my burned mouth. "The rule is that we stay next to the plane."

He looked back at the plane which was still burning. "It doesn't look like there's any plane to stay next to."

He was right. Almost nothing remained of it except the seat and yoke which his body had shielded from the flames. The emergency locator was melted, as was that entire section of the plane. There was nothing here for anybody to come to. "You're right," I said. "I don't think anyone's going to find it." Pain rocked me again, my entire body shaking in the incredible agony. "Terry," I said, "what do I look like?"

He avoided the question at first, which scared me. "Terry, please, what do I look like?"

"You look like a baked apple," he said.

My heart skipped a beat. "What's a baked apple look like?"

"Your face is all red and swollen, and the skin is cracking in places. The cracks are white, and parts of your face and head are black."

"I'm scared," I said.

I felt a tightness around my waist and upper legs where parts of my pants still clung. I looked down and saw that my body was swelling, and my pants were stretching tight around the ballooning areas. "I'm in trouble, Terry. I've got to get down off this mountain."

"I know."

He suddenly jumped away from me and yelled for me to hide. He ran and hid behind a rock.

"What's the matter?" I called out, fumbling over rocks, trying to follow him.

"The hissing. Can't you hear it? It's going to explode." He pulled back behind the boulder.

I ran and hid behind a tree, but nothing happened. I heard the crackling of the burning plane, but other than that everything was muffled by the heavy fog. "There's no hissing, Terry," I said. Either he was going crazy or I was going deaf.

It was several minutes before he came back to me. "I don't know what it was," he said, "but it's gone now."

What was happening? I was sure there hadn't been a hissing sound. But the excruciating pain from my burns could have made me miss it. "Terry, I've got to get down off this mountain. I've got to get help."

"Okay," he said. "You've always been the spiritual one. Say a prayer for us first, then lead us down."

"Okay." I closed my eyes and tried to concentrate on something besides the pain. "Heavenly Father, help guide us down this mountain. Amen."

The pain was crushing me now, driving me insane, and I began running down the mountain. I had no shoes, no coat, no shirt—only jeans, my underwear, and the carpet remnant melted to my chest. My feet stung every time they hit the ground, and sharp, jagged rocks tore at what was left of them.

I moaned in anguish with every step, but I kept moving, beginning to chill from the cold. It had begun to rain and slush again, making the rocks slicker and the mud deeper.

Soon my weight tilted forward, and I ran faster until I knew I was running too fast, but the pain was chasing me, filling me, becoming every thought, and the next thing I knew I was falling forward, slamming against a rock, glancing off another, somersaulting over the granite blades and coming to a crushing stop against a waist-high granite boulder. I knew instantly that I had hurt myself. My hip felt dislocated. I tried to get up but couldn't. I looked at my right leg. Blood was dripping freely onto the ground, and even some of the burns were bleeding now, torn open by the fall. Fog enshrouded me on every side. No movement, no sound. I had no idea how far I had run or how far behind Terry was. All I knew was that I was in incredible pain and no one was near and the fog and slush were getting colder.

I took a deep breath and almost gagged on the pungent aroma of sage. The rain and slush must have intensified it because suddenly the acrid odor was all I could smell. Sagebrush was all around me, short, scruffy silhouettes in the ghostly fog, silent spectators to my suffering. I sat in the mud, holding my bleeding leg in my hand, and began to cry.

"Thumper! Thumper, where are you?" Terry called from somewhere up on the mountain. Thumper was a nickname he had used since we were married, but I hadn't heard it much lately.

"Thumper, where are you?"

"Crying," I called out.

He came nearer, and I saw his form through the fog. "Crying?" he asked. He stood next to me. "What happened?"

"Please, Terry, just get me off this mountain."

"Can you walk?" Then he saw my leg, and he knelt and put his arms under me—careful not to use his burned hands—and lifted me into the air. He smiled as I lay my head against his arm. "Never mind," he said, "I'll lead."

I knew he was strong—he'd been a wrestler in high school—but his strength surprised me. I weighed over a hundred pounds, and he carried me like a doll. I tried to help by holding onto his shoulders and neck to lessen the burden, but I don't know if he needed it. He stepped carefully down the mountain, at the same time watching for the rocks that lay in his path. Gradually we wound our way down, slipping in mud or on rocks but never falling. He was in control at that moment.

A putrid, nauseating stench suddenly hit us. Terry stopped and carefully lowered me to the ground. "What is that?" he asked.

Something was lying on the ground ahead of us, but the fog was too thick to make it out. The stench seemed to be coming from there, so I leaned on Terry and hobbled as we cautiously made our way toward it. When we were ten or fifteen feet away I knew what it was.

"It's a deer," I said. "It's been ripped open."

There were large cat tracks all around in the mud.

"There's a mountain lion around here," I said. "We must have scared it off." Steam rose from the flayed entrails of the deer, still moist and hot. We looked around, each in different directions, but saw nothing. The lion may have been able to see us, but we couldn't see it.

I thought of my own trail of blood and smelled the sickly sweet odor of my own burnt flesh. "Let's get out of here," I said. "I don't want to be anyone's dinner." Terry and I looked around once more before heading down the slope again. I tried to walk by leaning on him, and soon the pain in my hip began to subside. The terrain was pretty smooth, no large gullies or ridges or monolithic rocks to navigate around. The slope was fairly steep in places but not so severe that we had to hold onto things to lower ourselves. The mountain itself was actually kind to us. Though we had no idea where we were or in which direction to go, we knew we needed to go *down*. Whatever it took to get down, we would do—and do it as fast as we dared.

The fog still covered us, limiting our vision to forty or fifty yards and muffling every sound. It was as if we were descending into an eerie, silent, lifeless crater on the moon. Even the sage seemed skeletal and dead. We had been walking for about an hour, when a new wave of weakness hit me. It came straight from my core, telling me I couldn't go on, buckling my knees, making me want desperately to stop. But I couldn't stop. I realized that if I stopped, I would never get going again. If I stopped now, it would be only moments before I sat down, and then it would be only moments before I lay down, and then only moments later, I would die. I knew it. But, I also knew that I couldn't keep going. Somehow, I managed to let gravity pull my left foot down another step. I balanced, then I let my right foot fall, balanced again and so on, letting gravity haltingly, agonizingly pull me down. I wasn't walking, I was falling step by step into the valley I hoped was below. I felt like I was dying with each little step, but my feet kept swinging out in front of me just in time to keep me from collapsing.

"Terry," I said, fighting to stay up with him, "don't let me die."

"I won't," he said.

"We need to get back to our children. We need to be there for them."

"We'll get back. Don't worry, RaNelle. We'll make it."

"Terry, we *need* to get back to our children. I know that. We can't let our parents raise them. We can't let anybody else raise them. They need to be our focus now. I don't care if we have any more big toys or fun things to do. I don't want another plane or fancy house or expensive cars or anything else. I just want to take care of our children. We need to be their parents. We need to love them."

"I know," Terry said, "I was just thinking the same thing. We need to change our lives, to make them our priority."

"Please, Terry, don't leave me."

"You'll make it okay, RaNelle. You're doing fine."

He pulled away from me a little; either he was speeding up or I was slowing down. I found that I could walk on my own now, but not as surely or as quickly.

"Terry, I can't keep up."

"Come on, RaNelle. You can do it. Just keep walking."

I was dying, and to my horror I knew that, somehow, *he* didn't know it. He pulled away from me a few more feet.

"Terry, I can't keep up."

"Sure you can, RaNelle. We need to get off this mountain. Just keep on coming down."

"But you've got shoes on. I can't keep up. Please, slow down."

"Come on, RaNelle."

It was like the hissing again. One of us couldn't comprehend what the other was experiencing. I hadn't heard the hissing; now he couldn't feel my fear or see my weakness.

My shoulders were tiring now, burning as if they had been holding weights, and I realized that I had been holding my arms out from my sides with my hands raised in air. My hands burned so badly that I couldn't stand the throb of the blood pulsing through them when they hung down. I lowered my hands to rest my shoulders for as long as I could stand it then raised them again like a scarecrow. The freezing mist, mixed with light snow now, seemed to diminish the burning a little. Terry had been walking quickly, and I had been trying to keep up. The burning in my foot intensified, and suddenly a large slab from the sole of my left foot fell off. I realized as it fell away that it had been flapping like a thong for awhile, but I hadn't distinguished it from the other pain. Now, raw flesh hit the rocks, and I tried to find mud to step in wherever I could.

Terry stopped, and I caught up with him. He was listening for any sounds from vehicles, equipment, something. But the world was silent. I found myself weakening again, my legs yielding to gravity and fatigue. "Please, Terry, let's go. I can't stop. I won't get back up if I stop." So we started down again.

I concentrated on the ground, trying to pick my steps around the sharper rocks. But now I was freezing. Why did my coat have to burn off? I thought. First I almost burn to death, and now I'm freezing to death. I looked up and saw Terry walking several feet ahead of me. His coat had been completely untouched by the flames. I realized now just how naked I was and how exposed to the cold, and I became grateful that I hadn't been able to pull the carpet piece off me. I held my arms a little lower and closer to my body.

"Terry, I'm cold."

"Come on, RaNelle, you can do it." He glanced back but didn't stop.

"You have a sweater on underneath your coat, don't you?"

"Come on, RaNelle. Keep going."

He pulled farther ahead, and I began to feel panicky. If he left me behind, I wouldn't make it. I doubted I would make it anyway, but at least I had a chance with him near me.

My feet were bogging down more than usual, and I looked down to see what was wrong. I couldn't believe my eyes. It was if I had shoes again. Huge, bizarre gobs of mud and clay had congealed around my feet in massive balls. The mud must have collected gradually after the slab of my foot fell off, but I hadn't noticed it. They felt like they weighed ten pounds apiece.

"Terry, look at this. Terry?"

I looked up and couldn't see him. Fog enveloped me on every side, leaving me a statue in a sea of gray, freezing nothingness.

"Terry!" I grew more panicky. "Terry!"

"What?" I heard his voice, but I could see nothing.

"Where are you?" I called out.

"Keep coming, RaNelle," his voice carried up through the rocks and trees. "Just come down the hill. I think it's getting flatter."

I tried to hurry, though the balls on my feet and my growing weakness made it difficult. But Terry was right, the slope was levelling out, and there were fewer rocks here. Maybe we were coming to the bottom of the mountain.

"Terry! Where are you?"

I heard his voice farther away. "This way," his voice said faintly. "I found a fence."

I tried to ignore my feelings of panic and pain, of isolation, and I concentrated on trying to follow his voice. A fence meant there might be a house nearby. Or, it might mean a ranch, or government property, or it might mean nothing at all. I had to find Terry.

"Terry! Please come back!"

There was no response. "Terry! Terry!"

I fought my fear and continued onward, finding level land and eventually the fence. Beyond it was a field of wheat.

"Terry!"

"This way, RaNelle! Follow the fence." The fog was a little lighter, and I could barely make out his form about a hundred yards away. I followed the fence toward him, telling myself not to stop, not to rest. Fear of losing Terry again in the fog motivated me to keep going. I tried to increase my pace, but I could hardly keep my balance now. We had been walking about two hours.

Terry was trying to pull the fence down. "We need to get in there," he said. He yanked again, but the fence was too strong. "Come on, help me."

I grabbed the wire but could barely pull on it. I think it helped me remain upright more than anything else.

"We'll have to climb it," he said and put his foot on the bottom wire. He steadied himself, then quickly climbed over. He looked at me from the other side. "Come on," he urged me. "Climb it."

"Terry, I can't. I can barely breathe. I can barely stand up."

"You've got to, RaNelle. It's our only way out of here. If you can get to the top, I'll catch you when you come down."

"What? How can you catch me?"

"Don't worry about it. Just climb up."

That fence might as well have been a hundred feet high right then. I looked at it and knew I couldn't scale it, probably couldn't even get to the second strand. But then I found myself grabbing it and putting my right foot on the first strand and gently pushing myself up. I put my left foot on the bottom wire and felt the fire of the line digging into raw flesh. I grabbed the fence post with my right hand and pulled my right foot up one more strand, then the left foot. The carpet flapped out and caught on a barb, and I had to balance myself while I worked to get it untangled. At last I found myself balancing on the top strand, the wire cutting into both feet and the carpet getting in the way of my arm.

"Jump!" Terry said. "Just jump on top of me."

I aimed right at his chest and let go. When I hit him I knew he couldn't catch me. His hands were burned worse than I had realized and were completely useless. He stumbled backward, but I stayed connected to the fence by a barb that hooked itself into my right hand. The sudden pain overwhelmed everything else and made me scramble to get my legs back under me. I stood up and saw a piece of flesh pulled partially away from the palm of my hand, the fence fastened to it like a meat hook. I screamed, and Terry pushed me back toward the fence to relieve the pressure on my hand.

"Terry, help!" Frantically, I worked at the barb, but it wouldn't let go, and finally, insane with panic and pain, I yanked my hand away, ripping the flesh off. Terry rushed up and saw the blood flowing from the wound and dripping to the ground.

"Raise it," Terry said, "and hold it with your other hand. Keep it above you so it doesn't bleed as much." I put my hand up and tried to hold it, but the carpet got in the way.

He looked at me a moment, wanting to help, but we both knew there was nothing better to do than to find help. He turned and started walking quickly toward an old dirt road that paralleled the fence. Several yards away another road veered off, and Terry stopped and looked down each. All we could see was fog in both directions. I prayed that he would make the right decision. He pointed down the second road and said, "Let's go that way."

"Why?" I asked.

"Because it feels right."

I wasn't going to argue. If it felt right, then we were taking it. Intense pain and fatigue were all I felt right then.

He took off, his hands raised to let the cool air fan his burns. He left me behind and I yelled for him to come back. He waited for me once or twice, just long enough to let me see him in the fog, then he took off again. My panic was giving way to anger now. How could he leave me? How *dare* he leave me? Bitterness welled up. Anger seethed, and as I shuffled along the dirt road I realized that I had more energy than before. The anger was invigorating me.

The fog lifted for a moment, and I saw something to my left. A house!

"Terry, come back! Civilization! I found a house!"

Terry came running back and stood with me a moment on the road. But what had looked like a house to me was really just an old outhouse. Weeds grew up around it, boards were falling off, and we could tell that it was obviously abandoned. I felt the energy slip away from me. "Terry, I'll just stay here anyway. You go ahead and get help," I said.

"No, you need to keep going. You need to come with me."

My breathing had become more labored the last few minutes, and I knew I had to sit down and rest. Something was terribly wrong inside. My throat was raw, and my lungs burned.

"Terry, I can't."

"You have to! I'm afraid I won't be able to find you when I come back."

"I can't breathe. I need to rest."

"No, RaNelle. You need to keep going. Come on. Let's go." He started off ahead of me.

I hated him. I was freezing, and my feet were filleted like raw salmon, and my hands were burned beyond recognition.

I couldn't breathe, the pain was incredible, and he wouldn't let me rest. He wouldn't help me. I wanted to hit him. I wanted to leave him. I wanted everything to be fair for a while. The rain and slush intensified, and I raised my hands to feel it, to let it cool and soothe my burns, then I started down the road after him. But he left me again, and I began crying. I felt the tears stinging the burns on my cheeks and chin. Terry stopped when he looked back and saw my face.

"Hey, RaNelle, think of the great story we'll have to tell our kids. Remember how our parents used to tell us how hard it was to walk to school? Two feet of snow, sixty below zero, five miles uphill, both ways. Remember that? Look what you'll be able to tell the kids."

I laughed a little. Yeah, this would be a story to top them all. I could tell them how Mom lost her face and hands because she didn't listen to that voice inside her. But right now I just wanted Terry beside me. Keep talking to me, Terry, I thought. Keep encouraging me. Tell me something else. I just want to hear your voice. I just want to know you're beside me. Please, Terry, talk. Talk.

He pulled ahead again, snow and mud flopping off his shoes as he walked in the washed-out rut. His shoes would probably get ruined, I thought.

I couldn't laugh again.

I forced my lungs to take short, quick gasps, squeezing all the air I could into them. I willed myself to breathe, to walk. Terry *wouldn't* leave me. I would keep up. I thought of the time I hiked to the top of Mount Whitney with no shoes on. I was ten and my brother Vincent was so impressed at what I had done that he took pictures of me to show his friends. He had a sister who had scaled the highest mountain in the continental U.S. in her bare feet. Of course, I hadn't wanted to.

My father had taken some of us out to the trailhead and started climbing. If we wanted to go, we had to keep up. For some reason I still had Sunday shoes on, and by the time we'd gone a mile or two I had wicked blisters on both feet. It was either go back alone or take the shoes off and keep going. I kept going. I walked over rocks, snowfields, gravel, but I made it. My father saw a glider that had crashed on the rocks below the peak, and he went down to see if anybody was still in it. The glider was crunched like a wadded-up ball of paper, but nobody was in it. They had already been taken out— dead or alive. Now I saw my father walking ahead of me. If I wanted to go, if I wanted to get there, I had to keep up. Come on, RaNelle. You can do it. My father's feet flopped in the mud ahead of me, fading away in the mist. My father had a coat on. My father flew the plane. My father was walking away from me.

I heard a noise. Something in the distance. Faint.

I stopped and listened.

"Terry," I called, "what's that? I think I hear a motor."

We listened but heard nothing.

The pain was driving me crazy. There was no escaping it, no ignoring it. I had to move to keep my mind on something else, to let the air flow over the wounds.

"No, there's nothing there," Terry said. "Let's keep going."

I was already walking. The balls of mud on my feet, like dark brown casts of plaster, were getting heavier. Even though they protected my feet, they weighed me down like diving weights. I tried to watch them with every step, to focus on their crazy, round appearance, but pain again interrupted me. My face and hands and thighs were on fire. My left foot was excruciating. I wanted to scream, to let go and burst my lungs with pain, but I knew I couldn't. I knew if I let down that last barrier of self-will that I would never regain it. My will was the only thing sustaining me now. I forced myself to hold the pain in, to breathe, to walk—to breathe, to walk. We had been walking three hours now, but it seemed like three days. I was beginning to weave, staggering, halting, then moving onward. I tried to walk straight, but my body wasn't responding. Deep-down, gnarled weariness was winning.

I saw an empty beer can on the side of road. I stopped and studied it. A beer can meant someone had been here, perhaps still was.

"Terry! There's a beer can!" I yelled. "Look for the drunk! Look for the drunk!"

Terry turned around and peered at me through the fog. I knew that whoever had drunk that beer was still close by. He had to be. "We're over here!" I shouted, throwing my head back and raising my voice as high as I could. "Please help us!"

Terry looked at me in sadness. "Come on, RaNelle," he finally said. "Let's go."

I stopped yelling and gazed at his face. Something told me he was right; we had to keep going.

We came to another barbed wire fence and got over it without incident. A recently cleared wheat field lay inside, and we tried to walk through it, but the stubble broke through the mud on my feet and became too painful to walk on. I moved over to the dirt road alongside the fence and kept to the mud. Terry came back and did the same. Soon he was lost in the fog.

Every step meant agony. Every step meant life. I couldn't go on, but I had to. I lifted my foot and put it down. The road was a blur. I didn't see fog anymore. I didn't feel snow or rain. I didn't hear myself breathe. I didn't think. Pain and movement were all I knew. One step, a Herculean task, was completed. Another begun. I lived for one purpose only—to keep myself from dying.

An eternity passed.

Something registered in my ears. A sound, something waking me up, bringing me back. Terry's voice.

" . . . a car. I think I found the road!"

Terry was so far ahead I could barely make out his words. But if he said what I thought he had said, then I knew he was dead wrong. I knew that we were both hallucinating, staggering under our weariness, seeing only what we wanted to see.

"I just saw another one!" he called back. "Cars! The road!"

His body, black against the gray mist, was moving now, waving at me. He acted as demented as I did when I saw the beer can. "There are no cars," I called to him. "You're hallucinating. It's just an illusion."

He looked back toward his illusion then turned back to me. "First one to the mirage wins!" And he ran into the mist. Silence surrounded me. Mist and silence.

I wanted to fall to the earth. Terry was finally gone.

But I found myself still alive, still walking.

My legs had become stiff, with my knees locked straight. I walked by rocking from side to side and bringing my legs out around me. My arms were virtually frozen in place by my head. I was like a machine, stiff, robotic, unyielding. I wouldn't give in. I was going back to my kids, no matter the price. I finally came to where Terry had been standing when he saw his mirage, and I stopped to try to find him. Dimly, something moved in the rain and fog. It looked like a man, like Terry. It looked like he was pulling up and down on something instead of walking.

A car flashed across my view.

It startled me. I took another step and tried to see through the fog more clearly. Another car flashed by, close to Terry, and I could tell now that he was yanking on another barbed-wire fence. Sounds came to me, and I heard the cars now. A truck roared by. Then more cars. This was real. I heard it. I saw it. Terry was actually pulling on a fence, and cars and trucks were streaking by.

We had reached the highway. But I had also reached the end of my endurance.

My steps had become mere shufflings, only inches at a time. It may have taken me fifteen minutes to go the forty or fifty yards to where Terry had been standing when I thought he was hallucinating. I began to stumble and knew with a deep, inner knowing that I had reached my limit. My will, and God, and Terry, had brought me this far, but I could go no farther. I tried to speak, but I didn't know how far the words reached. "I can't make it," I said, and I felt myself falling.

Chapter

F I V E

T ERRY RAN TOWARD ME, AND SOMEHOW HE CAUGHT ME before I hit the ground. I took another breath and tried to bring my feet under me again. "Terry, take care of the kids," I said. "I can't make it."

He held me up. "Come on, Thumper, breathe," he said. "We're almost there."

My throat was swelling shut from burns suffered when I inhaled the flames, and each breath required terrific effort— each literally a breath of life. I caught another ragged breath, squeezing it through my swollen windpipe, and I steadied myself.

Holding me around the waist, Terry helped me over to the fence. With every step, my body wanted to sink into the earth, and every time I looked down to see if I was still walking, I was surprised. I leaned against a wooden fence post. It was just a scraggly little juniper limb, hardly enough to lean against, but the fence itself was solid. Terry and I were amazed at the tension in the wires. He had spent ten or fifteen minutes trying to push it over or tear it down but couldn't. And he couldn't climb it because the wires were thinner than the other fences, and the barbs were closer together. Three strands of wire ran parallel to the ground, and a fourth zigzagged in diagonals across them. The bottom strand was too low to crawl under, and the top was too high to climb over, and the zigzagging strand prevented the possibility of crawling through. Whoever had built it didn't want anybody getting in; unfortunately, nobody could get out either.

"Start waving your arms," Terry said. "Maybe a car will see us and stop." He was kicking a fence post as hard as he could but the fence barely trembled. I propped my arm on top of the weather-beaten juniper branch and tried to wave. Terry gave up on the fence and began hollering and waving his arms.

Looking at the road I noticed that there was another fence between us and the highway. I couldn't believe it. There were *two* fences. Both identical. And between the two fences ran a dirt frontage road—two fences and another road to get over before we could reach the highway. I tried to breathe, to keep standing, to keep waving. I couldn't give up now.

A car approached with a young couple inside. The woman was looking out the window, and the man was driving. As they passed, she saw me, and her eyes opened wide. She quickly turned and grabbed the man's shoulder. I saw him shake his head no, and the car continued on. I was devastated. How could they ignore a man and woman screaming for help on the side of the road? Who could see somebody burned as badly as I was and not help? We yelled and waved for ten minutes, then fifteen minutes, and nobody even slowed down. In spite of the fog, I knew that many of the people saw us. Anger filled me, and I shouted at the passing cars. As one vehicle after another passed by, I became livid.

"If I live through this," I said, "I'm never helping another person again. If I see somebody who needs help on the side of the road, I'll aim right for them. I'll be the first to hit them."

Terry looked over, dropping his arms momentarily. "Hang in there, RaNelle. Somebody'll stop." He raised his arms again to wave.

"I don't know how much longer I can do this, Terry. It's getting harder to breathe. I'm scared. I can hardly stand up."

"Come on, RaNelle, you need to keep waving. Keep trying."

A large, loud semi truck came toward us from the south, going a little slower than the other vehicles, its engine straining to pull its load. I saw a large black man, maybe in his thirties, in the driver's seat, and I stared into his eyes, willing him to look at me. His head turned, and seeing me, his eyes grew wide. His head turned to the side to watch me as he went past.

"He's the one, Terry! He's going to stop."

But the truck continued and disappeared into the fog. Terry slowly shook his head, disappointment appearing on his face. "Keep waving," he said.

A loud screeching sound came from the north. Moments later we heard a low growl as the truck backed its double trailer toward us. When it came into view, the truck stopped, and the man's face appeared at the passenger window. He stared at us for a second. The door flew open, and he ran up to the first fence. He stared at us again, maybe thirty feet away.

"Is this a Halloween trick?" he asked.

I wanted to hug him, and I began crying.

"No," he said. "We've been in a plane crash and need help."

He looked at me again, just staring, and I could see the horror on his face. It was the first of many times that I would experience that look from others.

"Yeah, okay," he said. "Just wait, I'll get to you. Just hang on." And like a maniac, he began tearing into that fence, literally ripping off some of the barbed wires. "Thank you, God," I said. I was praying and crying and trying to breathe, and I knew that I was going into shock. I began shaking, quickly losing control of my body. My self-will, which had supported me to now, was breaking down. Another car came up and parked behind the truck—a sheriff's car. I was overwhelmed with gratitude. We were going to make it. The sheriff stepped from the car and walked around the front of it, eyeing us carefully. Then he pulled his gun out. I watched in disbelief as he leveled the gun at us and came forward.

"No, please," I heard myself saying. "We've been through enough. Don't shoot us."

The truck driver stopped working on the fence, and the sheriff stepped off the road and came near him, turning his gun on the truck driver. "What have you been through?" the sheriff said, eyeing the truck driver but talking to us.

The truck driver took his hands off the fence and backed up a step or two. He had suddenly become very cautious.

"We've been through a plane crash," I said. "We need help."

"Well, I got reports that there was a hold-up. Truckers are calling in saying somebody was holding up a man and a woman by a fence here."

I could see how someone would get that impression. Terry and I had been standing with our burning hands raised in the air.

"No," I said. "He's helping us. We need to get out. Our plane's back up on the mountain."

The sheriff, seeing the situation clearly now, put his gun away and went to the section of fence the man had been beating on. "Come on, help me," the sheriff said. "Let's get them out of there." Together the two men shoved the fence post with their feet, trying to push it over. They kicked at it, but the thing was stronger than both of them. They kept at it and after about five minutes they had bent the metal post enough that the truck driver could climb over while the sheriff held the wires down with his foot. The man ran across the gravel road between us and came to our fence.

"You're really hurt," he said, looking at me. "We need to get you to a hospital right away." He kicked the fence post but it didn't budge. So he stepped on the lower wire and pulled up the wire above, creating an opening about eighteen inches tall. "You gotta crawl through," he told me.

I numbly stared at it. With the carpet sticking out on both sides of me, I wasn't going to get through very easily. He strained and pulled the opening a couple inches wider, and I slowly got to my hands and knees.

"Come on, lady. You need to get through here."

My hands flared in agony the moment they touched the ground. I hesitated, knowing I would get caught on the barbs.

"I can't keep holding this," he said. "Come on through."

Terry stood next to me, holding his hands in the air, waiting for his turn. When I tried to put a leg into the opening, I saw just how much it had swollen. The fluids in my body had been pooling to the surface to hydrate the burns, and I was bloating like a balloon. My pants, what little was left of them, caught on the barbs, and I was stuck. Then the coat remnants on my back got stuck and the carpet also got snagged. I couldn't move, and the barbs began cutting into my skin. A slice of my Levis tore away, exposing a large blister on my thigh. It ripped open and fluids drained into the burns next to it. The pain was excruciating, and I began to feel panicky again. Terry reached down and ripped the last of the coat off my back and yanked the carpet free of the fence and helped me through. As I rose to my feet, I wavered a moment, then saw that I had lost most of my clothes. Parts of my pants and burnt coat hung from the fence, and the rest, I assume, had vanished in the fire. At least I had my underwear and the carpet remnant to cover me. Fortunately my undergarments, and all the skin under them, had been untouched by the flames. Terry scrambled through the opening, and the truck driver, our angel of mercy, let the wires snap shut.

The driver helped me across the road to the second fence, but I had no strength left. The sheriff pushed the fence down with his boot and held his arms out to me. I tried to inch up to the fence, but I was literally out of energy. The truck driver and Terry pushed me from behind, the sheriff grabbed me from the front, and they hoisted me over the fallen fence. Disbelief was written over the sheriff's face as he set me down and looked at me. "An ambulance is on the way," he said.

He rummaged frantically through the trunk and rear seat of his car and emerged with a blanket that looked as though it had been dragged through the mud behind a truck. I could hardly open my eyes now, but I saw that the blanket was not something I wanted to put on my raw flesh.

"I'm sorry," he said, "I had to use this in prisoner transport last night, and it's not very clean, but it'll keep you warm." He held it out and threw it on my shoulders. I screamed in pain.

"Get it off! Get it off!" I shouted, trying to get it off without touching it with my hands. I twisted and the blanket fell off. He wanted to help, but there wasn't much he could do. He stood, looking helplessly at me as I stood on the side of the road trying to keep my hands in the air. "I'm sorry," he said. "I'll call and see why the ambulance isn't here yet." He walked me over to the car and opened the passenger door.

But as he was about to help me into the front seat, I saw my reflection in the side mirror. The horror of my image will stay with me forever. It was nothing like what Terry had described. My face was burned almost completely black. Blood oozed from several cracks, flowing down to the gap where my chin used to be. My face and head were swollen almost out to my shoulders on both sides. Even my ears were hidden in the bulging flesh, and my eyes were nothing but blackened slits on my face. My hair, once long and blond, was incinerated to black, crispy clumps along the top and sides of my skull. The sight was hideous and I screamed and screamed in uncontrollable horror.

My emotional pain had collided with all the physical pain, and I became lost to it. I looked in the mirror and saw this beast's frenzied screaming, and the beast was me. The hysterical, bellowing creature was me.

It was me.

I put my hand to my head and pulled off a clump of melted hair. I put a finger to my face and it stuck to the melted flesh that had once been a cheek. I pulled my finger free and brought burnt tissue with it.

The sheriff wheeled around and tried to pull me away from the car, but I was glued to the hellish visage in the mirror— an image I would never lose. The mirror would stay in front of me for the rest of my life, my hair coming off, parts of my face sticking to my finger, my screams of terror echoing in my ears.

The sheriff put his arm around my back and tried again to guide me away from the car. I found myself going with him, screaming with every breath, seeing nothing, feeling nothing but my inhuman face.

"Come here," he said. "I want to show you something."

He pointed to a large green sign in front of us. I made out the words: Fillmore—1 mile.

"Do you realize that if you had kept walking along this fence, you would have come right to the doors of the hospital? It's right off this exit, one mile away."

He continued, "You must have been led here. You're so close to the hospital that any second now you're going to hear the ambulance start up."

At that very instant an ambulance siren wailed in the distance, coming from the direction of town, but I was still crying, holding my hands to my face, wanting to deny everything that was happening to me. The sheriff walked me back to the car, and the next thing I knew an ambulance was beside us and I was being lifted on a stretcher into the back of the vehicle. People tried to take my hands away from my face, but I wouldn't let them. My arms were suddenly like steel; my face didn't exist. My face didn't exist.

Then blackness came.

Chapter

S I X

SOBBING WOKE ME. SOUNDS OF GRIEF, OF DEFEAT. I HAD heard the voice before, but never like this, never in such sorrow. His cries came from beside me, but when I tried to open my eyes to look at him, I couldn't. My heart filled with sympathy for him. It's okay, I wanted to say, "Don't blame yourself, Terry. I'm going to be okay." I opened my mouth to speak, but nothing came out.

I became scared. Why couldn't I speak? Why couldn't I see? His sobbings continued, as if he couldn't see my struggles. I opened my mouth again and forced a guttural noise out—an inhuman sound. It burned my throat to let the air pass through. I made the noise again, but the sobs continued. Terry couldn't hear me.

My arms were at my side, and I used my hands to feel gently around. Pain shot through them, but by barely touching things I made out my surroundings. I was on a hospital bed, lying on my back. A light sheet covered my chest. The carpet remnant had been removed and my upper chest stung as I lightly traced my finger across it. I reached for Terry, but couldn't find him.

Pain filled my body and seemed to emanate from me like an aura of electricity. Pain filled the room, my face, my hands, my arms, my feet, my legs, my throat.

I heard another voice, a young man's, and Terry stopped crying. I heard a curtain screech on a metal rod as it was pulled to a side and then pushed back again. I realized that Terry had been behind it. He hadn't been able to see me. The young man spoke to me from near my feet, but I couldn't respond. He moved my foot, but I couldn't feel the touch of his hand.

"This mud is like a boot," he said, and I realized that the mud balls were still on my feet. I heard the scrape of a chair as he sat down and the clank of a pail of water as it settled on the floor. Moments later he was washing my feet, trying to scrape the mud off. Another man came in and touched my right leg. Speaking briefly to the first, he began cutting away at the jean remnants.

"Oh, no," I heard him say. "The skin has melted to her pants. I'll have to cut into her leg." And after a pause I heard a ripping, cutting sound, but felt no pain; the cutting of skin gave no greater sensation than that of the burns. He finished the cuts, expressing some surprise that I wasn't burned beneath my underclothes. I felt exposed, but there was nothing I could do. They didn't even know I was conscious.

"Oh, no," he said again. "Look at her hands. They're black. There's been no circulation. Get the doctor."

"What'll they do?" the first man said.

"Probably have to amputate. See how the tissue is already cracking; it's dead. And look at the bone here, near the first finger. See how it's been burned through? Fourth degree. The bone is completely dissipated. Better get the doctor in here."

"No!" I squawked—a hideous crackly sound. I was terrified. "No! No, you can't take my hands off!"

"We're getting the doctor," the second man said. "Just lie still and try to be calm. We don't know what's going to happen yet."

The fire in my throat was intolerable, but I had to communicate. "You can't take my hands! You can't amputate them." I swung my head back and forth—the only movement I could make.

The doctor came in and held my right hand. The pain flared anew as he touched the raw areas. He went to the other side of my bed and held my left hand. "Tremendous swelling," he said. "Fluids are settling in the hands and lower arms. It doesn't look as if there's been any circulation for . . . what's this?" He was holding my left hand, pulling at it, digging into my fingers. "Her rings are still on," he said, almost in disbelief. "They've constricted the blood flow until her fingers have . . . Quick! We've got to get them off." He pulled at the ring, trying to slip it off, but the finger was more than twice its normal size. The skin and outer layers of tissue were gone—he was pulling the ring against raw nerves, muscle, and tendon. I thought I would pass out again from the pain. "We've got to get this ring off," he said. "Maybe the circulation would increase and we could save her hand, at least this one, if we can get it off." Then, in holding my wrist, he felt something else, something buried deep in the ballooning flesh.

"Her watch is still on!" he said. "Scissors!"

He dug the scissors down into my wrist and probed and gouged until he got the blade under my leather watchband. I screamed and tried to break free, but they held me down enough to make the cut, and the watch came off. A tremendous surge of blood and pain shot into my hand, and I screamed again.

"We've got to get that ring off," he said. "Check and see if she has any others." I did. One other ring on my right hand.

He began digging into my finger to try to cut the ring off and I heard him say, "Be careful. Can't cut the finger off."

"No!" I screamed, but I could barely make my voice heard. "Don't cut my finger off! Don't cut my finger off!" He dug the scissors in deeper, and I became hysterical because I thought he *was* cutting my finger off.

"We can't get it off, RaNelle," he said. "I'm going to call in a jeweler and see if he can cut it off."

"Don't cut off my fingers!"

"We're trying to save your fingers. If we can get those rings off we might be able to save both your hands as well."

The jeweler arrived shortly and explained to me that he was going to cut my rings off with special cutters. After a pause—during which I imagine he looked at my charred and swollen head, my lacerated arms, the bare, blackened flesh of my gnarled hands, knowing that he had to hold them to work on them—he took my left hand and "snip-snip," the wedding ring was cut in two. Then with the cutters he pulled the pieces out of my skin. The intense heat had melted the gold onto my finger. The diamonds were lost—they had fallen out when the mounting melted—but that was the least of our worries. He took the other hand and cut that ring off. The whole process took less than a minute and was less painful than anything the doctors had done.

The men left the room, and some female nurses came in. I heard water again and managed to ask them what they were doing.

"We're going to wash you," one of them answered, and I felt warm water flow over my legs. "This is a saline solution. We've got to clean those burns before infection sets in." The salt water felt like alcohol on the burns, but I was almost too weak to scream.

"We know this hurts," one of them said, "but we've got to do it. Just hang on, RaNelle."

"Can't you give me a painkiller?" I managed to ask.

"We already have, honey. You've got a shot of pure morphine in you."

"I still feel like I'm on fire."

"Nothing can stop the pain," the nurse said. "There aren't any painkillers invented that can stop the pain of a burn. You'll just have to go through this."

It felt like they were rubbing the skin off my body as they washed. I clenched my teeth and tried to pretend that the pain wasn't mine, that the arms and hands and face they were cleaning were somebody else's. But there was no pretending.

Others came into the room, and I heard whispering men's voices. It was the doctor and the other men who had been working on my legs and feet. I could hear "she" this, and "she" that, but nothing else. Then they came nearer, and the doctor spoke louder.

"RaNelle, uh, this isn't normally what we do, but, there's something we need to discuss with you. We feel you ought to know what we want to do." He was nervous, hedging about something.

He explained that I was going into hypothermia and that their facility wasn't equipped to deal with injuries like mine. I would have a better chance if I went to the regional burn facility in Salt Lake. It was three hours by ambulance, but less than an hour by helicopter.

"No!" I screamed "No plane!"

"It might make the difference," he went on. "It could save your . . ."

"No! No plane. I'm not getting in a plane. Never!"

"What's going on over there?" Terry's voice said from the other side of the curtains. "What are you doing to her?"

They opened the curtain and began whispering to Terry. I

grew panicky again. They wouldn't get me in another plane, or a helicopter, or anything else that left the ground. I'd die first. A bizarre story came to mind about a helicopter that crashed in the mountains. One of the survivors pulled the other crew members out, then radioed for help. Another helicopter came and loaded him and the injured men in, strapping him to a gurney because he was injured too. As they took off, the side door opened, and his gurney fell out. He began rolling down the mountain, screaming for help, but the helicopter was already leaving. Then he watched as the helicopter suddenly spun out of control and crashed. His gurney jolted to a stop against a rock. He broke free and made his way to the crash site, only to find that everybody had been killed.

"No!" I screamed. "I'm not getting in a helicopter!"

"RaNelle," one of them said, "it's for your own survival."

"No! No! No! I'm not flying ever again." And I screamed as loud as my raspy, scratchy, burning voice would let me. And then I heard Terry join me as loud as he could, both of us screaming at the top of our lungs:

"No plane! No plane! No plane!"

"Okay, okay," said the doctor. "We'll get an ambulance, but we need to hurry. Nurses, get her ready. Get her things. Quickly. Let's get her out of here." Everyone snapped into action, but suddenly I was absolutely fatigued, deeper than I had yet felt. They asked me questions, but I couldn't answer. I was still wet from the saline solution, and they covered me with sheets. I was cold inside and on fire outside, but I didn't have the power to speak. I was slipping away.

They loaded me into the back of an ambulance, and I heard an I.V. bottle rattle in behind me. A male technician and three female nurses got in, then Terry, and they closed the doors. They crowded around me, hooking me up to a heart monitor and to the I.V. They put oxygen tubes into my nostrils, and the ambulance drove off. There were six of us crowded into the back of the little, hearselike ambulance. I thought Terry was sitting next to me until I heard him call for more morphine, then I realized he was down by the door. He could still feel the fire in his hands and thought more morphine would deaden it. They gave him another injection. He still complained of pain.

I was really struggling now, fighting for breath. It took all the energy I had. My chest wouldn't expand like it needed to bring in air. It was as if a large weight was on my chest, and the weight was growing heavier with every breath. About twenty minutes into the ride I reached deep inside for all the energy I could muster and tried to force out the words: "Help. I can't breathe." The male technician put his face near me and said, "What?"

"Help," I whispered, not knowing where the strength came from to say it. "I can't breathe."

"Stop trying," he said. "We'll do the work for you."

Oh, thank you, I wanted to say. I felt so relieved that I could stop trying, that I could finally stop fighting, because I was weary to the bone. It would feel so good to rest a few minutes. Perhaps he only meant that he would put the aspirator all the way down my throat and force my lungs to breathe and that I could stop trying *then*, but what I heard was: "Let go, RaNelle. Stop fighting." And so I did, and a sudden release swept through me, and I was relieved of all pain.

Suddenly I could see. Whatever he'd done had allowed my eyes to open. I felt stronger and more clear minded. I could see all the nurses as they rushed around the gurney in a commotion. I thought something had happened to Terry, that they were working on him, but then I saw him sitting in the back of the vehicle below me. One of the nurses took a large, plastic bulb in her hands and began pumping it, like a bellows, and Terry said, "What's wrong? What's wrong?" And somehow I could sense his feelings, as if they were instantly communicated to me. He felt guilty. He thought he had killed me, that I was dying from my injuries in the accident and that it was his fault. But why couldn't he see that I was all right now? I could sit up and see what was going on. Oh, he's doped up, I thought. It's the morphine. He's not thinking straight. He can't see that I'm okay. But then the thought hit me: how did I get next to Terry in the ambulance, and why was I sitting up so high? And why was I so incredibly alert and clear minded?

What on earth was going on?

WE'RE JUST CLEARING HER LUNGS," ONE OF THE NURSES said to Terry. "It's just a little congestion." I watched from my place near Terry as she pumped the plastic bulb while the others helped the young man work on the person on the gurney. Terry sat back against the side of the car and smiled from ear to ear. His feelings changed completely, and the morphine began taking over. A silly smile was stuck to his face and I knew with absolute clarity that the morphine was controlling him now.

But what was happening? Who were the nurses working on?

Suddenly I began to feel afraid. Immense blackness flooded over me like a rapid, dense fog. The darkness was so absolute that nothing was visible, and it seemed that nothing ever could be visible in it. Then, just as suddenly, bright, vivid lights began flashing around me, psychedelic lights that were brighter and more colorful than anything I had seen before. I looked down at myself, and in the brilliance of the lights saw that my body looked perfectly well again. No burns, no bleeding, my hands and feet were whole. I stood in the midst of a spectacular light show, feeling absolutely whole and complete. But my fear remained. I must be dreaming, I reasoned. I knew I had been burned; my hands had almost burned off, but now they were perfect in front of me. I was dreaming.

Or, no, it was the morphine. I'm having a psychedelic trip, I thought. I've been overdosed like Terry, and my mind is playing tricks on me. But would I be able to reason so clearly if I were having a drug-induced trip? Would I be so self-aware? And so aware of others—their thoughts, their feelings? I was experiencing something more real than anything I had ever experienced. So, if this wasn't a dream or a trip, what was it?

At that moment I was sucked into a narrow tube, and I began flying through it feet first. The tube was extremely tight, and I became more frightened because it almost felt like my body was being sucked inside out. My speed was tremendous—indescribable. Nothing on earth has ever gone that fast, nothing could. It felt as if I were whizzing past galaxies, but the colors and lights were right next to me, almost brushing against me, and my fears mounted.

Then I heard voices. It seemed people were traveling beside me somehow, although there was no room for them. I became aware of one person near me who was alone and not speaking. I couldn't see anyone; I just knew the person was there. Then I heard two men speaking, also traveling beside me, and I knew they were speaking about me. I focused on their voices and was able to make out their words, but they were speaking a different language. I heard everything they said, and I seemed to recognize the language, but I couldn't comprehend what they were saying. *What is that language?* I asked myself, getting frustrated because I knew that I had heard and understood it at one time. *Why can't I understand it now?*

The voices stopped and a brief scene flashed before me. A series of pictures, words, ideas, understanding. It was a scene from my life. It flashed before me with incredible rapidity, and I understood it completely and learned from it. Another scene came, and another, and another, and I was seeing my entire life, every second of it. And I didn't just understand the events; I *relived* them. I was that person again, doing those things to my mother, or saying those words to my father or brothers or sisters, and I knew why, for the first time, I had done them or said them. *Entirety* does not describe the fullness of this review. It included knowledge about myself, that all the books in the world couldn't contain. I understood every reason for everything I did in my life. And I also understood the impact I had on others.

A part of me began to anticipate certain events, things in my life I would dread seeing again. But most of them didn't show up, and I understood that I had taken responsibility for these actions and had repented of them. I *saw* myself repenting of them, sincerely wanting God to remove the weight and guilt of those terrible actions. And he had. I marvelled at his sublime love and that my misdeeds could be forgiven and removed so easily. But then I saw other scenes that I hadn't anticipated, things that were just as awful. I saw them in horrible detail and watched the impact they had on others. I saw that I had let many people down in my life. I had made commitments to friends and family that I had just let ride until they were irreversibly unfulfilled. People had depended on me, and I had said, I'm too busy or it's not my problem, and just let it go. My cavalier attitude had caused real pain and heartache in others, pain I had never known about.

I was shown a friend who I knew had suffered terribly in her life. She lived in a beautiful, spiritual world before she came to this life, and she had been confused and hesitant about coming here at all. But she was given the promise of good parents, family members, and friends, and she agreed to come for the experience and growth this life would afford her.

I was shown that I was one of the key friends who had been given to her as a guide and help. Then I saw my own personal follies and uncaring attitudes. I saw how these had combined to mislead my friend and propel her into new mistakes and grief. I had messed up my own life, not really caring about the consequences, and in so doing had hurt her as well. If I had followed through on my obligations to myself and others, she would have lived an easier and more productive life. Until that moment I had never realized that ignoring responsibilities was a sin.

What was happening? Why was I seeing all this? My mind spun with questions.

Next, I saw a woman whom I had been asked by our local church leader to visit periodically. I was just to check up on her and see if she needed any help. I knew the woman quite well but was afraid of her constant pessimism and negativity. She was locally renowned for her bitterness. I didn't think I could handle the depressing influence she would have on me, so I never went to see her. Not once. I saw now that the opportunity to visit her had been orchestrated by higher powers, that I had been just the person she needed at that time. She didn't know it, and I didn't know it, but I had let her down. Now I *lived* her sadness and felt her disappointment and knew I was a cause of it. I had fallen through on a special mission to her, a responsibility that would have strengthened me over time. I had retreated from an opportunity for growth, both for me and for her, because I was not caring enough to fight through my petty fears and laziness. But the reasons didn't matter; I could see that, even now, she was living in sadness and bitterness, living through it just as I now experienced it, and there was nothing I could do to go back and help.

I re-experienced myself doing good things, but they were fewer and less significant than I had thought. Most of the great things I thought I had done were almost irrelevant. I had done them for myself. I had served people when it served me to do so. I had founded my charity on conditions of repayment, even if the repayment was merely a stroke to my ego. Some people had been helped, however, by my small acts of kindness, a smile, a kind word, little things I had long since forgotten. I saw that people were happier because of my actions and in turn were kinder to others. I saw that I had sent out waves of goodness and hope and love when I had only meant to smile or to help in a small way. But I was disappointed at how few of these incidents there were. I had not helped as many people as I thought.

As the review of my life came to an end I was in agony. I saw *everything* I had ever done in vivid, immediate detail—the bad things, haunting and terrifying in their finality, and the good things, ringing with greater reward and happiness than I had ever imagined. But in the end I was found wanting. I found *myself* wanting. Nobody was there to judge me. Nobody had to be. I wanted to melt in the agony of self-indictment. The fires of remorse began to consume me, but there was nothing I could do.

The scenes of my life were gone, and the colored lights returned.

Was this all a dream? It had to be. The dark tube seemed to tighten against me as I flew through it, faster and faster.

"Wake up, RaNelle!" I told myself. "It's a dream! Wake up." But I continued on, sailing through the dancing lights of unreal colors, oblivious to direction or destination.

A dot of light appeared far off in front of me. It was just a pinpoint, a tiny speck in the distance, but its brilliance distinguished it from all other lights around me and I instinctively pressed towards it. Emanating from it was a love and hope and peace that my soul hungered for. I *wanted,* I *needed* this brilliant, radiant light. The black tube took the shape of a tunnel now, opening up as I neared its end. The light burst forth before me, filling everything with brightness, and I was coming upon it impossibly fast. Oh, my gosh, I thought, it's brighter than the sun. It'll blind me! It'll kill me!

I remembered my burns from the plane crash and was afraid they would ignite again in this radiance. But I couldn't stop myself. I was drawn to the light by forces I could not control, so I shut my eyes against my impending destruction. But my eyes wouldn't shut. They felt shut—but somehow I could still see. And then I was in the light.

Like a nuclear explosion, the light pierced me. Every particle of me was shot through with blinding, brilliant light, and I had a feeling of transparency.

My skin didn't burn. My eyes still saw. I floated in this light, bathed in it, and the love that surrounded me and filled me was sweeter and finer than anything I had ever felt. I was changed by it, refined, rarified, made pure. I basked in its sweetness, and the traumas of the past were far behind me, forgotten and transformed by peace. Then an image appeared in the distance.

A woman walked toward me dressed in white. Her hair was white, and her face shone with light. I had no fear of her; the love I felt allowed no fear. She came forward and stood immediately before me. Then she smiled, and I loved her smile. It filled me with even greater love, and I wanted to know her. She spoke my name.

"RaNelle."

But her lips didn't move. Her smile never changed and my first thought was, "Wow, what a trick! Her lips didn't move."

"RaNelle," she said again, and I realized her voice sounded in my mind and not in my ears. How could this be?

"RaNelle," she was more insistent. "It's Grandma."

And the moment she said this, I recognized her. She was my mother's mother. But she looked different than I had remembered. She was full and rounded and vibrant. She appeared to be about twenty-five years old, but her hair was glorious white, and everything about her was radiantly beautiful. Her body was glorious, and I began to understand why I hadn't recognized her. She had been frail and sick all the years I had known her. Then the realization hit me.

Grandma was dead; she had died a couple of years before. And I thought, if she's dead, then what am I doing here?

Oh, I'm dead.

The thought came out of me like spoken words, though I hadn't moved my mouth.

Now everything fit. The colorful lights, the life review, and now this light of glorious love, all of it naturally occurred as my life continued in this next world. This definitely wasn't some dream or some drug-induced vision. I was more keenly aware and alive now than I had ever been in my body. I immediately accepted this, and wanted to know where everybody was.

Grandma giggled. Her lips didn't move, but her spirit giggled.

"Aren't people supposed to meet me when I die?" I asked. "Aren't there supposed to be people singing hallelujah and coming up to hug me and saying, 'Welcome'?"

She giggled again, and I thought it was the most delightful giggle I had ever heard. "Well," she said, "everybody is quite busy. Come on. You have a lot to see," and she reached out for my hand. But I thought, "Wait, what about Jim?"

Jim was a friend who had been killed in an automobile accident several months earlier. If Grandma was here, maybe she could tell me what happened to him. "What about Jim?" I said again, and then I saw him in the distance, walking toward us. Instantly I wanted to run and embrace him, but my grandmother put out her arm and said, "No, you cannot."

I was startled. There was a power in her words, and I knew I couldn't oppose them.

"Why not?" I asked.

"Because of the way he lived his life," she said.

He had come closer now and had stopped ten or twelve feet away. He was dressed in jeans and a blue shirt that was unbuttoned to mid-chest. This was how he normally wore his shirts on earth, but I thought, my goodness, that's risque. Do they let you dress like that in heaven?

He smiled, and I could feel his happiness. Although he didn't possess the same kind of light or power that my grandmother did, he seemed content. He gave me a message to give to his mother, asking that I tell her to stop grieving over his death, to let her know that he was happy and progressing. He explained that he had made certain decisions in life that had hindered his growth on earth. He had made the decisions knowing they were wrong, and now he was willing to accept their consequences. When he was thrown from the van that he and his wife and a friend had been in, his head had hit a rock, and he had been killed instantly. When he got to the other side, he was given a choice to stay in the spirit or return to earth. He could see that his growth on earth had come to a stop and that if he returned he might lose even that light which he had gained. So he chose to stay. He asked me to explain this to his mother, and I said I would, not knowing how I would accomplish it since I had no thought of going back myself. Then he said that he had a lot of work waiting for him, and he turned and left. I could tell that he was very busy, very engaged in matters that were vital to him, that would help him, though I didn't know what they were.

I looked at my grandmother and asked why she had prevented me from embracing him. She explained that this was part of damnation.

I was taken aback.

"The powers we are given," she explained, "are self-given. We grow by the force of our desires to learn, to love, to accept things by faith that we cannot prove. Our ability to accept truth, to live by it, governs our progress in the spirit, and it determines the degree of light we possess. Nobody forces light and truth upon us, and nobody takes it away unless we let them. We are self-governed and self-judged. We have total agency. Jim decided to limit his growth on earth by rejecting things he knew were true. He hurt himself and others by using and selling drugs. Some of the people were hurt severely. He had various reasons for turning to drugs but the fact remains that he knew these things were wrong. He chose darkness over light often enough that he would not choose light again. And, now, to the degree that he became spiritually dark, he is consigned to a similar degree of darkness—or lack of light—here in the spirit. Yet he still has agency. He can grow. He can still find all the joy he is willing to accept, all that he is capable of receiving. But he knows that he does not have the same powers to progress and achieve joy that others with more light have. This is a part of damnation, because his progress is limited. But he is choosing to grow. And he is happy.

"The Lord never gives more challenges in life than can be handled," she continued. "Rather than jeopardize someone's spiritual progression or cause more suffering than can be endured, he will bring that spirit home, where he or she can continue progressing."

All of this rang utterly true to me. She had communicated it with lightning speed, faster than computers can talk. It was instant and total knowing. I found that Grandmother and I could think on several levels at once and communicate them all simultaneously. You can't know something without knowing everything around it, what causes it, what sustains it. Knowledge dovetails in the spirit world, each piece fitting with other pieces. Every fact connected to it is seen instantly, in totality. We have nothing like it on earth. We can't even approach it. Our knowledge and ability to communicate is like a child's who hasn't yet learned a language. We struggle to communicate, but we don't possess the tools. We're like little children.

My grandmother held out her hand and said, "Come quickly."

I reached out to take it and stopped.

"Wow," I said. "Look at my hand."

My hand was clear, like transparent gel, but there was light coursing through it like clear blood. But, the light didn't run in irregular patterns as it would in veins; rather, the light shot through my hands like rays or beams. My whole hand sparkled with light. I looked down and saw that my feet also sparkled with light. And I noticed again that they weren't burned. My feet and hands were perfect and whole. They radiated this glistening, beaming light, and I looked at my grandmother and saw that her light was brighter than mine. Every part of her was more brilliant. Even her dress was glowing white. And I recognized the dress. It was the dress that she had been buried in. My mother had bought it for her funeral. I thought about what Jim had been wearing, and I understood that people there wear what they want to wear. They wear what they're comfortable in, and I knew that my grandmother must have loved this dress my mother bought for her. Although she had never worn it in life, Grandma was wearing it now, and she was radiant.

Moments later we were walking, holding hands, and the most beautiful panorama I had ever beheld opened before us.

Chapter

E I G H T

A GARDEN CANNOT EXIST ON EARTH LIKE THE ONE I SAW. I had been in gardens in California that had taken my breath away, but they were struck into insignificance by the scene before me now. Here was an endless vista of grass rolling away into shining, radiant hills. We have never seen green in our world like the deep, shimmering green of the grass that grew there. Every blade was crisp, strong, and charged with light. Every blade was unique and perfect and seemed to welcome me into this miraculous place.

Profusions of flowers were splashed on the hills in colors I had never imagined. Flowers of all sizes and forms—living, radiating, glorying in their beauty—erupted from the hills and valleys without end. The colors were indescribable. We may have fifty or a hundred tints of orange in this world. In that one there are millions. I saw tinges of orange that defy comprehension. Shades of rose and hints of pink stretched on forever, every subtle shade a unique color, every color connecting in perfect harmony with other colors, and every arrangement a miracle. Our colors all seem to be grays and browns and blacks in comparison—dead, drab, everything a muddle of the same staid tints. Even our brightest colors are artificial. There, colors vibrated with life, creating subtle shades of mood and atmosphere. The colors did more than please me, they infused me with happiness in their completion, in their wholeness. It was as if every blade of grass, every flower, every tree, had a unique prism from which light and spirit exploded.

And the whole garden was singing. The flowers, grass, trees, and other plants filled this place with glorious tones and rhythms and melodies; yet I didn't hear the music itself. I could feel it somehow on a level beyond my hearing. As my grandmother and I stopped a moment to marvel at this magnificent scene, I said to myself, "Everything here seems to be singing," which was woefully inadequate to describe what I felt. We simply don't have language that adequately communicates the beauty of that world.

I noticed something unusual about the flowers near us. My grandmother waved her arm and, without speaking, commanded them to come to her. Although it was a command, the flowers took joy in obeying her. They floated through the air and came to a stop, suspended within the circle of her arms. The bouquet was alive. Each blossom was able to communicate, react, and actually enlighten others near it.

"Grandma," I said, "they have no stems."

"Why should they have stems?" she said. "Flowers on earth need stems to receive nourishment, to grow to their fullest potential. Everything God has made is spiritual and is designed to grow towards its own spiritual potential. A flower reaches its fullness in the blossom. Here everything exists in its fullest form. These flowers have no need of stems."

"But they just float."

"Should they fall? Everything here is perfect." She took one of the flowers and handed it to me. "Isn't that beautiful?" she said.

The flower hung inside my cupped hands, barely touching me. It was like a camellia except that it was deeper than any camellia I had seen, and it had many fine tendrils at its center, some long and straight, others coiled. The petals cascaded one upon the other in luminous hues of lavender, orange, and pink. The whole blossom was filled with various shades of light, and its beauty was incredible. Then the flower became part of me. Its soul merged with mine. It experienced everything I was doing, or had done before. It was acutely aware of me, and at the same time it changed me with its delicate spirit, with its own existence and life. It affected my feelings, my thoughts, my identity. It was me. I was it. The joy that came from this union was more pervasive and delicious and fulfilling than any I had known until that moment, and I wanted to cry. The scriptures say that one day all things shall be as one. That statement has great power for me now.

My grandmother commanded the flowers to return, and they floated gently back to their places just above the ground. The one in my hands also returned, but its essence remained with me. Maybe it was this lingering connection with the flower that made me more keenly aware of my surroundings, but I began noticing other things. I saw large, powerful trees, and I understood that a tree reaches a fullness of creation in its growth and firmness. Unlike some flowers, the trunk of the tree, or its stem, is vital to its identity, to its spiritual fullness. The trees were similar to palmyra trees that grow in the tropics—only much larger. I sensed their intelligence, and the limit to that intelligence, and I knew that reaching their full height and width and firmness actually gave meaning to their existence. Their trunks were their foundation, and their leaf spread and total size was, in effect, their glory. The trees produced a scent that reminded me of something bouquetish, very flowery. Then I smelled another scent, a mixture between sweet pine and lilac. It came from a large, stately tree that reminded me of a pine tree but was fuller.

The sky above the trees had a lavender hue that seemed to turn blue in places where the light was greater. As I stood reflecting on all this, letting the entire scene permeate my being, my grandmother spoke again.

"All this comes from God, and the power to sustain it comes from him. It is the power of his love. Just as the plant life on earth needs soil, water, and light for nourishment, spiritual life needs love. All creation springs from God's love, and everything he creates has the capacity to love in turn. Light, truth, and life is all created in love and is sustained by love. God gives it love. We give it love. You give it love. And thus creation grows. And, RaNelle," she said, "I love *you*!"

As she said the words, I felt her love charge into my being, filling me with incredible warmth and joy. This was life. This was true existence. There had been nothing like it on earth. I felt the plants loving me, the sky, the fragrances, everything. And as I received my grandmother's words and this love, I knew that now I would be responsible to increase and heighten all love around me, whatever my circumstances. She was teaching me love, its definition, its extent and power, not just so I could take pleasure in receiving it, but so I could express it to others. I was being filled with love in order to become a source of love.

My grandmother took my hand, and as we walked through the garden she explained some of the basic purposes of our life on earth, the need to live the golden rule, the need to help others, the necessity of a Savior, the need to read scriptures and have faith, and I said, "Grandma, I already know this; I learned it all in Sunday school. Why are you teaching it to me again?"

She spoke simply, "It is within the simple principles of the gospel that the mysteries of heaven are found."

What was she saying? I couldn't see any mysteries in her words. I felt her immense love, but I could see no purpose in teaching me principles that had come clear to me years before. Yet she continued, reiterating the importance of basic goodness, religion, the power of repentance, things anybody can learn in the Bible. I listened, my frustration growing as we walked up the side of a hill. We came to the top, and I said, "Grandma, I know all that. I really do. Teach me more."

"You're not ready."

"Yes, I am, Grandma, I'm ready for much more."

"No, you don't believe the basics yet. You lack faith."

"What is it I don't believe? How do I lack faith?"

Oh, but she knew me. She knew me better than I could have imagined. As we stood on the bluff overlooking a small valley, I saw a scene that changed me forever. The scene was sacred beyond words, beyond expression, and those who have witnessed it keep it hidden in their hearts. I saw that I had indeed lacked faith, that love isn't simply a word or an emotion; love is a power that gives action to all around it. *Love is the power of life.* This was a turning point for me, something that allowed all of my understanding and love to magnify, but I can never share the details here except to say that I know that love between people here can be eternal. I felt Grandma beaming with happiness. I had passed a test.

Grandma took my hand, and we traveled quickly over the landscape. I looked down at the ground flying under us. We streaked like a beam of light across this immense spiritual world then moved upward into space, traveling even faster. Floodgates of knowledge opened, and truth poured into me without end or constraint. Its source was the light and truth all around me, and it was clarified, or explained at my level, by my grandmother. She gave me knowledge about God, life, the creation of the world, and even the reaches of eternity. The truths were comprehensive and complete and rushed upon me in such enormous volume that I thought my head would explode. It was coming too fast. I wanted to be able to absorb it, to remember it all, but it was too much. "I can't take this!" I said. "Stop!"

Instantly all communication ceased, and we came to a standstill. My grandmother looked at me and I *felt* her surprise. "Why are you doing this?" she asked.

"I can't handle all you're giving me. How can I possibly retain it all?"

"RaNelle, don't worry about it," she said to me. "Let go of the fear. Don't doubt yourself. You will recall things as you need them, and they will be brought to your memory by the Spirit. Have faith. Believe in the power of God."

Then I understood what had become the greatest block to my growth in life: fear. It had plagued me all my years, had stopped my progress, cut short my attempts at working through problems. Fear had limited my enjoyment of life and it was blocking me now. When I feared, my powers of travel, understanding and progression became paralyzed. "Don't fear this," I said to myself. "Let go." And we were traveling again, knowledge pouring into me faster than ever.

Scene after scene of living truth passed through me: history on earth, history of our existence before earth, principles, facts, things that I had had no conception of. I saw them. I experienced them, literally becoming part of each scene.

I saw that we all stood before our Father before coming to earth, brothers and sisters in eternity. I experienced this anew, just as I had experienced it in my own pre-mortal life. I saw that we chose to come here, to face trials and to gain the experiences of this earth. I saw that we elected to follow a Savior who would redeem us from the sins of our mortal lives and bring us back to our Father. I felt love and joy sweep over me again as we accepted Jesus Christ as that Savior. Then we raised our right arms, just as we might in a court of law, and we made a sacred covenant with God that we would do all in our power to accomplish our missions on earth. And I felt the tremendous honor of making this covenant before our Heavenly Father. We vowed, in effect, to become partners with him in bringing about goodness on earth. We promised to use our time and energies and talents to help bring about the Savior's full purposes, to help bring our brothers and sisters back to him and to our Father again.

I saw that our God knew each of us individually. He knew our hearts, our souls, and he loved us unconditionally. It was as though he spent unmeasured time with each of us, counseling us, loving us. Time did not exist; each of us had always had a relationship with him.

I saw that the people standing beside me on that occasion were people who would play an integral part in my life on earth. We were connected to each other in vital ways. If one of us were to fail in his or her mission, all of us would be hurt in some way. If one succeeded, we would all benefit. It was as if we were part of a puzzle with millions of pieces. It was put together perfectly, but if one piece were removed, we all would be lacking and would not be content until that piece was found and returned to its rightful place. We needed each other. We still do, and always will. I believe that it is impossible here to imagine the grief of a brother or sister who is lost from that grand family organization.

Many other events of eternity passed through me. I seemed to bathe in them, to *become* them. They were infused into my soul. And I know that all this knowledge is with me yet, some of which I remember, such as making the covenant with our Father, and some of which I am waiting to remember.

I asked my grandmother if I could visit my friends, the ones I had cherished throughout eternity. She said some of them were still on earth and that I would not be able to see them. I asked for the others, and instantly they came to me, beautiful people of light and love. I remembered them and their names. Some had already lived on earth and died, and some had not yet been born. All the memories of my existence before earth came back to me, but I was told that I would not retain them, that they were for this place only. I accepted that, and my friends came and embraced me, welcoming me back.

"We've always been with you, RaNelle," they said. "We've never left you. Oh, we love you so much." Incredible joy filled me as I felt their own joy at being with me again. Each person was individual and unique. Each had a different personality. I could sense a difference between the ones who had been to earth and those who hadn't. Those who had been on earth were discernibly brighter, more mature. But we were all, in that moment, like giddy children reunited after years of being apart, each of us sharing our experiences while I had been gone. Then I knew that some of them had been with me in spirit while I was on earth. They had comforted and guided me. I remembered a time when I was nine or ten. I had gone to my bedroom after being chastised by my parents, feeling hurt and alone, and I didn't want to live anymore. I was lying on my bed, praying for God to take me away, when I felt the embrace of two people around me. So much peace came into me at that moment that I didn't question the reality of it. Now I saw the two who had done this. They smiled, reminding me of the moment. I wouldn't call them guardian angels; they were friends, and they had always been my friends no matter the place or time. They had been to earth before me.

The younger spirits, the ones who hadn't been to earth, were then called away. They seemed younger only because they hadn't gained the experiences of earth life yet. We all looked the same age, somewhere in our twenties. After they were gone, the rest of us spoke on a higher level, sharing things we could not share with the others. Life on earth does something to us. It strips away a naivete, an innocence, and infuses our eternal selves with maturity and wisdom. With the others gone, we could now bare all of our lessons and experiences from earth. We looked forward to the future in a way we hadn't before, knowing better what the whole plan entailed.

My grandmother was getting anxious. There was so much to do, so much to learn, and there was only limited time to do it in. "We have to move on," she said.

"But I want more time with my friends," I pleaded.

"No, RaNelle, we must go. You haven't learned everything you came for yet."

My friends embraced me again and committed to stay with me. I felt their perfect love and knew they would never leave me. One female friend lingered and embraced me for a long time. She seemed bonded to me in a unique way, but I didn't quite understand what it was. "You know I've always been with you," she said. "I've never left you. And I never will." She hung on every word I said, and I was moved as I recognized her passion to be with me, her absolute devotion and love. "I'll always be there," she said again.

My grandmother took my hand, and we found ourselves in the garden again, traveling above another beautiful hillside. Everything was harmonious, perfect, like sweet music.

"I love you, RaNelle," she repeated over and over, her love for me coming in waves, like a sweet aroma, touching and filling every part of me. I never wanted to live without her love again. It seemed to give me life. "I will never leave you," she continued. "The Spirit will comfort you, be with you, and will allow me to be with you too."

Then she said, "Come. You must learn humility." And we came to a strange building below us. It had four walls, but no floor or ceiling. We could see partway down into it, then the room's light seemed to fade where the floor should have been. The walls were solid but translucent, as if they could be penetrated by light—or, rather, by beings of light. This seemed important.

I saw stairs leading down into a dark area. My grandmother told me to follow the stairs down into the room.

Somehow I sensed a deeper darkness. "No, Grandma. I don't want to."

"You need to," she said. "This is important."

"Can't you come with me?"

"I cannot."

I realized that there are laws in that world, just as there are laws here. This was a law she could not break: I had to go alone.

I started down, and the stairs seemed to disappear so that I gradually descended, or floated, into the room. The light was much dimmer, and I became frightened, though I knew that the light in that room was brighter than sunlight. At first I thought the room was empty, then I saw her.

A beautiful woman lay on her side on an altar. Behind her and to the sides hung broad scallops of fine scarlet fabric. Her head was propped on one hand, and her thick dazzling black hair fell across the front of her neck. She had an olive complexion, smoother than cream, lips full and exquisitely formed. Her eyes, a stunning blue, were set in a flawless face that looked as if it had never seen a harsh moment. Her fingernails were long and delicate, appearing to have never experienced work. Even her feet were beautiful—slender and soft; and I noticed that her toenails were perfectly groomed.

Gold and brass bracelets adorned her ankles and wrists in the style of her time on earth. A necklace of gold and brass hung about her neck, with a large ruby just above her breasts. Her blouse was crimson and partially sheer. It hung loosely from her shoulders and tucked into her waist. The front of it was open, slightly exposing her breasts and midriff. Her legs were draped in the same fabric. She looked about the room with an air of supremacy. Even in this realm of absolute beauty she was stunning.

I understood that she had been a queen, a woman of power and title who had lived before Christ and had reigned over many people. In life she had done as she pleased, commanded populations, granting or taking life, enjoying every whim. She had cultivated her beauty artfully and had used it to increase her power.

She looked at me and I knew that she expected me to bow, to honor her, but I refused; something told me not to. Her air of dignity unruffled, she looked about the room again as if expecting others to show obeisance, to show me how to reverence her beauty and power.

She was caught in a delusion. The room was deserted—there were no others—yet she believed there were multitudes surrounding her, bowing and giving her glory. I began looking at her with pity and sadness. Then I was shown that she had lived her life in selfishness and greed, that she had never given kindness for the sake of being kind. She had never given anything of herself, and now she was caught in eternity, in love with herself, smiling benevolently upon her invisible subjects, basking in honor and adulation that didn't exist. She was queen to nothing but her own vanity.

Her self-delusion was so complete that I began to fear being in her presence. I feared her sickness, the smugness, the self-glory, the darkness of her deception—and I cried out for my grandmother.

"Come, RaNelle," I heard her say, and I glided up out of the roofless room and back to the garden. My grandmother took my hand. Her touch and the beauty of the garden were like spiritual balm.

"Did you see?" she asked. "Did you learn?"

"Yes," I said, grateful to be out of the room, but aware also that I had seen a potential for delusion in my own soul. "Thank you."

We didn't speak of it again. There was no need. The image of the woman, once a queen on earth, now a figment of vanity, was seared into my soul. I could not escape the lesson she invoked. Even now when I see vanity, I feel a sadness for the person displaying it. I want to wake them up to what's real about themselves—their inner beauty, light, and love. My grandmother saw the impact of the lesson upon me, and we moved on, traveling with great speed again over the garden, which seemed to stretch for thousands of miles.

She waved her arm, and we stopped above another high hill, and I saw millions of people before us. "These are the spirits of those that have died," she said. "They are waiting for the work to be done. They're waiting for those on earth to finish their part of the work."

"Their part of the work?" I asked. "What work?"

She showed me that the people were organized into family units. "You committed yourself to giving your time and talents on earth to further the work of the Lord. You need these people, and they need you. We are all dependent upon one another."

My life review had already pointed out how remiss I had been in serving others. Now I saw that there was much I could do, sharing, sacrificing, offering what I have. The spirits of those who have died are waiting for each of us to come closer to the truth, to become part of the complete puzzle again, to recognize the divinity of God and live in his light.

Before moving on I saw that each person wore clothing from his or her own time period on earth. As with my friend, Jim, they wore what they were comfortable in.

We continued on and Grandma showed me the importance of being a mother and the value of the things I did for my children. I saw that my sacrifices for them had not been in vain. Although I had considered myself an unsuccessful mother, in reality I had helped my children more than I realized. I was shown the difference between men's and women's roles, both on earth and hereafter, and I saw things that changed my views on equality and fairness. I have always loved my womanhood, but now I love and honor what I can do as a woman. I don't need to do what a man does to have meaning in life. Womanhood gives me the same eternal significance as manhood gives to men. By fulfilling and magnifying my roles as mother, wife, daughter, sister, friend, I will gain the most glorious rewards possible. For both genders, loving and helping people is the key.

Grandmother then showed me much of my past again, this time focusing on my poor self-esteem. I hadn't loved myself, and this affected the way I had treated others. "You must love yourself before you can love others," she said. I viewed mistakes I had made as a mother due to my lack of self-esteem. I had lost my temper and hurt my children unjustly. I wanted to hurt myself but instead had hurt them. "Remember," she said, "that each child is a child of God. They are your spiritual equals. They have a life on earth as precious as yours, and they need your help. It's your obligation to give them as much knowledge as you can. Feed them truth. Give them experiences for their growth. Learn to love yourself, RaNelle, and you will love your children more."

Then she showed me how to love myself more. I needed to feed myself knowledge and truth, to study in my fields of interest, even going back to school if necessary. I also needed to pray more, and I was surprised when I saw just how little I had prayed in life.

"Pray as a mother," she said. "Pray to know how to raise your children, and your prayers will be answered. Read the scriptures. They are filled with truth. Study them, and you too will be filled. Answers will come. Wisdom will be added to you. You will feel the Spirit and come closer to the Lord."

She was preparing me for what I was about to see, though I didn't know it.

Grandma waved her arm and the ground opened before us. I looked and saw a person lying on a hospital bed surrounded by doctors and nurses. The person's face was bandaged.

"You will never be the same, RaNelle," Grandma said. "Your face will be altered and your body filled with pain. When you go back, you will have years of rehabilitation . . ."

"When I go back?" I looked at her. "You expect me to go back?" Sudden understanding came, and I looked at the person on the bed. The arms were spread wide, and both arms and hands had been sliced in several places to allow the fluids to drain into plastic bags.

"Is that me?" I was horrified.

"Yes, RaNelle, it is you. You will be badly scarred . . ."

I became frantic. "Grandma, I'm not going back."

"Your children need you, RaNelle."

"No, no they don't. They're better off with someone else. I can't give them what they need."

"It's not just your children, RaNelle. You have things to do—things that aren't finished yet."

"No, I'm better off here. I don't want to go through all that." I pointed to my body. "I refuse. I want to stay here."

I sensed my grandmother's awareness that time was growing short. "You *must* go," she said. "Your mission isn't complete."

"No, I'm not returning to that body! I'm not going back."

In response, my grandmother swept out her arm and commanded: "Look!"

A rift opened in the space before us, and I saw a young man walking toward us. At first he didn't seem to understand why he was there. Then he saw me and looked stunned.

"Why are *you* here?" he said almost in disbelief. As I remained silent, his disbelief changed to grief, and he began crying. I felt his grief, his sadness, and I too began crying.

"What's the matter?" I asked. "Why are you crying?" I put my arms around him, trying to comfort him.

"Why are you *here*?" he repeated.

Then I understood that my refusal to go back to earth was causing his sadness. I belonged on earth *for him*, I understood, and I immediately felt guilt for my selfishness.

His name was Nathaniel, and he hadn't been born on earth yet. He said that if I didn't go back, his own mission would be hindered. Then he showed me his mission, and I saw that I was to open doors for him, to help him, to encourage him.

"I will complete as much of my mission as I can," he said, "but I will never fulfill it without you. I need you."

I thought my heart would break. I was a part of his puzzle, and I was hurting him and everyone he would help by refusing to go back to earth. I felt a great love for this young man, and I wanted to help him in every way I could.

"Oh, Nathaniel," I said, "I swear to you that I will help you. I will go back, and I promise that I will do everything I can to do my part. I will open those doors for you. I will protect and encourage you. I will give you everything I have. Nathaniel, you will complete your mission. I love you."

His grief was replaced with gratitude. His face lit up, and I saw the great spirit he was. He was crying now with gratitude and joy.

"Thank you," he said. "Oh, I love you."

My grandmother took my hand and drew me away. Nathaniel watched me leave, still smiling, and I distinctly heard him say, "I love you, Mom."

My spirit was thrilled, but I couldn't respond to him, as things began happening very quickly. "RaNelle," Grandmother said, "there is one more thing I need to say to you. Tell everybody that the key is love."

"The key is love," she repeated.

"The key is love," she said a third time.

Then she let go of my hand, and the word *love* reverberated in my mind as I left her and fell into a deep blackness. I was crying as I left the world of light and glory and love.

The last thing I saw was her outstretched hand.

Terry and me on one of our first dates in high school, a New Year's Eve dance. We were married two years later.

When I saw this photo for the first time, I was amazed. Although I didn't see it until after my accident, I instantly recognized my grandmother, Annie Bronson. Here, she is in her late teens.

My grandparents, Annie and Clinton Bronson, at their 50th anniversary celebration. Grandma passed away shortly afterwards. She served as my guide in the most precious and beautiful experience of my life.

Thanksgiving 1984 at home in Bakersfield. Exactly one year later I would be coming home for the first time from the hospital. Christina and Jason are waiting for their share of the turkey.

Terry and the kids with his mother, Ruth Wallace. This was taken one week after we bought the plane.

Our "beautiful, immaculate death machine" moments before leaving Rialto for Salt Lake City. In the photo on the right Terry is rearranging the luggage. My mother was crying as we pulled down the runway. She too knew that something terrible was about to happen.

"Thumper" saying hello upon arriving at the Rialto Airport. This is the door that never stayed closed in flight—and wouldn't open during the crash. Christina is also waving hello in the rear window. My brother VaLoy took the photo. You would never know it from this picture, but I had just written my last will and testament.

At left, two views of the crash. After the accident, Federal Aviation Administration officials went up to the mountain and studied the crash site. The sheriff who had helped us at the road led them up, following directions given by Terry. The sheriff found a camera in the rocks and took these pictures with it. The camera had been thrown from the plane and had partially melted, but still worked. The two rectangular frames in the bottom picture were the pilot's and passenger's seats. The long, twisted wreckage jutting out from the seats towards the edge of the photo is the wing I crawled on during the fire.

The "indestructible" fence where Terry and I waved for help, one mile south of Fillmore, Utah. We walked out of the mountains (shrouded in clouds in this photo) and then trudged across these fields.

With Jason, pointing at an airplane flying by, April 1986. For years the sound of an airplane overhead would excite Jason and he would run to point at it. Now he wants to be a pilot. The graft on my arm came from the skin on my stomach. (Photo by Casey Christey)

At the Mayor's Eagle Award Reception in Bakersfield, 1986. I'm talking to Patty and one of her daughters. Their home and possessions were destroyed in the house fire, but the family was safe. I'm wearing the Jobst mask and gloves.

I wore the Jobst mask for a year and a half; then I wore this clear plastic mask for another six months. This picture was taken two years after the crash.

At the California State Fireman's Association Medal of Valor Awards, in 1986. I was more concerned that night about my bandaged hands than about the award they'd given me. I'd just had more surgery on both hands. For weeks afterwards I couldn't perform the simplest tasks, and from then on I only had surgeries on one hand at a time. I stopped keeping count of the surgeries after my twentieth operation.

On the mountain again, years later. Terry and the children are holding pieces of wreckage they found in the rocks. Near here I found a small pile of change that had once been in my purse.

The swath the plane made through the brush is visible over Christina's right shoulder.

Newsweek magazine asked me to pose in front of Patty's house, which had burned down three days before. The newspaper article in my hands is the one that started the flood of donations that helped us in our plight.

This letter from President Reagan gave me a lot of hope and encouragement—once I read it. At first I thought it was an advertisement from Westinghouse and I threw it in the trash. Fortunately, Terry spotted it and suggested I take a closer look. I was deeply moved by the President's words, especially his belief "that our Lord will give [me] the strength to meet each challenge." I have always found that to be true.

THE WHITE HOUSE
WASHINGTON

April 16, 1986

Dear Mrs. Wallace:

I have recently learned of your act of heroism in helping your neighbor and her children escape from a fire. While this in itself would be considered courageous, it is especially commendable that you would do this in light of your own bad experience in a fire prior to the rescue. I am pleased to join the members of your community in commending your bravery and your determination.

Although you have had many difficulties, I believe that Our Lord will give you the strength to meet each challenge. With the love of your family and your gallant spirit, I have no doubt that you will find your way to happiness.

Nancy joins me in sending our prayers and our best wishes. May God bless and keep you.

Sincerely,

Ronald Reagan

Mrs. RaNelle Wallace
3301 Shiloh Ranch Road
Bakersfield, California   93306

NINE

PAIN HIT ME LIKE A TRAIN. MY ENTIRE BODY, FROM HEAD to foot, reeled in agony. I heard two doctors discussing my condition: the nurses had lost my pulse in the ambulance but had kept aspirating me en route to the university's Intermountain Burn Center in Salt Lake City; I was hooked up to life support and given an EEG, but it was registering only sporadic activity.

"Maybe we're not getting a clear reading on her brain waves because of the swelling around the cranium," one doctor said.

"It's possible," the other said. "There are three to four inches of swelling. Do you want to try again?"

"No, let's just keep monitoring her and see what happens. Her uncle, Mr. Woodruff, was just here and, surprisingly, she's showing improvement now, but it's doubtful she'll make it through the night."

My mind reeled. What were they saying? I wasn't dying. I had already done that and had come back. "I'm alive," I wanted to shout, but the pain consumed all my energy. I couldn't move, couldn't speak. And what was it they had said about my Uncle Woodruff?

Later I learned that after the hospital called my parents, Mom had phoned my aunt and uncle in Brigham City, Utah, and had asked them to be with me until she and Dad could make the trip from California. After my aunt and uncle arrived, my uncle, Ivan Woodruff, was allowed to spend a moment with me alone. Uncle Ivan is an Elder in his church and had wanted to give me a priesthood blessing to help me recover. He laid his hands on my head and felt impressed to command me, in the name of Jesus Christ, to be healed and live. The moment he did so my body literally jumped several inches off the bed. The monitors went crazy, he said, all of them beeping and chirping, except for the heart monitor, which went blank. Seeing it go blank, he thought he had killed me. Nurses rushed in, and he stepped away, beginning to cry. Clumps of skin from my head had stuck to his fingers. My head, he said later, had felt like a large, burnt marshmallow.

"I'm sorry," he had said to the nurses. "What did I do? Did I hurt her?"

A doctor checked first me and then the machines. Evidently the heart monitor had come unplugged when my body jumped. The doctor plugged it back in, and my heart registered again.

"Did I hurt her?" my uncle asked again.

"No, Mr. Woodruff," the doctor said. "This is the first positive sign we've had since she's been here. Look at this printout—her signs went below the chart for a second there, and now, see, they're all higher. We've got signs of sustained life. Whatever you did, it worked."

My uncle left the room, and this is when I became aware of my surroundings and heard the doctors discussing my condition. I heard one of them say that he was on his way to see Terry, who was in another room undergoing treatment for burns on his hands. After checking the monitors one more time, he left. The other doctor remained with me.

Some time later my uncle returned with my aunt, Carol. She shrieked when she saw me, and I heard her say, "Oh, no," over and over. "Look at her. Oh, please, no, look at her. She can't live. Her head's wider than her shoulders. She can't live." Moments later she was unable to bear seeing me and had to leave; then I heard my uncle's voice.

"Doctor, do you think she's going to make it?"

"I don't know," he said. "She's extremely weak. With all the fluids rushing to her burns, she's suffering dehydration, and the swelling is putting a lot of pressure on her brain. I don't know. We've placed a shunt in her skull to drain the fluids, but it may be too late. If she lives, she may never regain the use of her body."

"You mean she might be a vegetable the rest of her life?"

"My best guess is that she won't pull through. I suggest you take care of the donor slips immediately."

"Can we sign them?" my uncle asked. "Or does her husband have to sign?"

"He's not doing too well himself," the doctor said. "He was given an overdose of morphine, and he still doesn't know where he is. He refuses to believe that his wife is badly hurt. He just says, 'No, she's fine. She walked off the mountain with me.' We've told him she may not make it, but he won't sign the papers. You better take care of it. She may pass on at any time."

My aunt was there again.

"Can you hear me, RaNelle?" she asked, rubbing my right arm on an area that wasn't burned. "RaNelle, are you there?" She spoke very slowly, making sure every word was clear. "If you can hear me, try to let us know. We love you, RaNelle."

But I couldn't speak. I couldn't move. Everything in my body was paralyzed. I wanted to talk to them with all my heart, to tell them where I had been. I wanted to share the wonder and happiness of that marvelous world on the other side. Besides the ever-present pain, that world was the only thing on my mind.

"Look at the monitor, doctor!" one of the nurses called.

The graphs on my monitor had jumped again.

"Carol," the nurse said, "speak to your niece again. Watch this, Doctor."

My aunt rubbed my arm again. "If you can hear me, RaNelle, please show us. Let us know."

"See, there it goes again," the nurse said.

"Looks like we've got a response," the doctor said. "Carol, she's responding to you."

"Fight, RaNelle," my aunt said. "We'll be with you. We'll take care of everything."

"Doctor," my uncle said, "can she hear us?"

"Yes," he said, "she probably can."

"Should we be talking about organ donor cards then, right in front of her?"

The room was quiet a moment.

"Hang in there, RaNelle," my aunt said again, still rubbing my arm. "We're with you."

Later that night I became alarmed as I heard nurses saying that I probably wouldn't make it through the night—certainly not for another twenty-four hours. I remembered hearing talk earlier of donor cards, and I became desperate. I wasn't enduring all this pain only to give up and die.

"Dear Lord," I prayed, "I know you didn't send me back to become somebody else's body parts. You sent me here to *live*. Now, please help me show them that I am alive—that I'm not going to die." And I began trying to move again, but nothing happened. I tried harder, and I felt something move.

I couldn't tell what it was, but as I tried again I felt the same movement.

"Her graphs are bouncing up and down," a female voice said.

I could feel the presence of a second woman come in and stand beside my bed. I could even feel her spirit, just as I had felt the presence of beings when I was on the other side. I tried to move again, and my whole body jerked. Wow, I thought, I made my body move! I summoned my strength and did it again.

"RaNelle," the new nurse said, "stop that! It doesn't help anything, and you're screwing up the machines."

No, I thought. I need to convince you I'm alive. I jerked again.

"Stop that, RaNelle!" she ordered. "Just relax."

I lay still. Had I convinced them? The second nurse left after a moment. I didn't hear her leave, but I knew her spirit had left the room. I lay there, seeing nothing but blackness, feeling enormous pain and wondering what would happen to me now. I prayed again.

Another nurse came in, and my heart jumped. What a spirit she had! Her presence was grand. I felt the strength and goodness of her whole person. She was an answer to my prayers. I tried to jerk my body for her, and instead I felt a strange motion in my arm.

My left arm had risen in the air and crashed on the bed. Oh my gosh, I thought. I just moved my arm! This is great! I lifted my arm again and let it thump on the bed.

"RaNelle," the nurse said, "are you okay? Are you doing this intentionally?"

I managed to make a sound, just a grunt, but to my ears it sounded like the finest, happiest sound in the world.

"Wonderful, RaNelle," she said. "You're there, aren't you?"

I lifted my arm again and grunted.

"RaNelle, let me get the doctor!"

She left and moments later returned with two men—the head doctor and a neurologist. I yanked my arm up and let it fall back on the bed. As I did this my body jerked again with the effort.

"No, no, no," the doctor said, and I heard him sketching on a pad. "Don't you know that when patients are dying they often experience severe muscular spasms? See the rigidity in her arms, the twitching of the torso? She will be dead in moments, if she isn't already." The doctor's voice sounded final. If I didn't know better, I would have believed it myself.

"Before you remove the I.V.s and life support," he went on, "be sure to tie her arms down. They could break something if not restrained." He wrote some more and added, "Keep monitoring her." The doctors left.

The nurse came near and whispered in my ear. "I don't believe him," she said. "I don't think you're about to die. I think you're trying to communicate. RaNelle, can you hear me?"

I jerked my body again.

"Listen, I've got an idea. I'll be right back." She left, and I tried to relax. I was excited—and grateful—for her belief in me and willingness to help.

"Okay," she said, coming in and sitting near me, "I want you to use your arm to spell out what you're trying to say. I'll write it down. Can you use your arm that well?"

I concentrated on lifting my arm and controlling it. I began writing the words I wanted to say.

A moment later she stopped me. "No, no, you're writing too fast," she laughed. "One letter at a time, okay?"

I held my arm up again and found it easier this time. I wrote the letter I.

"Okay," she said.

Then I wrote A, then M.

"Okay," she said, "'I am . . .' what?"

I wrote D.

Then Y.

Then I, N.

"No, no," she broke in. "No, RaNelle, you're not dying. Hang in there. You've made it too far. You've survived a plane crash. Your husband's alive. Come on, RaNelle, life is worth fighting for!"

I raised my arm again and spelled N, O.

"RaNelle," she plead again, "you can't give up now. I won't let you! You've come this far. You're going to live!"

I raised my arm again and spelled N, O, I, A, M, D, Y, I, N, G, F, O, R, A, C, O, K, E.

"Oh!" she started laughing. "You just want a Coke?"

My arm was getting tired, but I raised it again. D, I, E, T.

She laughed and other voices joined in. "Well, she's obviously okay," the head doctor said from the doorway. "She has process of thought," the doctor who had condemned me said. "I'd say she's going to make it."

"Treatment begins first thing in the morning," the head doctor added. I learned later his name was Doctor Saffel. "Let's work towards getting her in the whirlpool as soon as possible."

I had gotten through to them, and my body parts would not go to someone else. And soon they would put me in a jacuzzi and make me feel better. Yes, I thought. At last. They believe me. I'm back.

My aunt and uncle thought my ears had been burned away the first time they saw me. Then they realized that my head had swollen so much that it engulfed both ears, completely covering them. My mouth and what was left of my nose were hidden in the folds of what had once been cheeks. Two puffy slits between folds identified where my eyes were hidden. A plastic tube snaked out of this round mound of swollen tissue, and my aunt and uncle couldn't tell if it went down the hole for my nose or mouth. This was my breathing tube. My throat had been severely seared and had swollen to the point that I could not draw air through it. So the tube was inserted into my mouth and down the back of my throat. It allowed me to live, but by morning the tube was literally killing me. It was clogged—I couldn't draw enough air through it.

I began squirming and trying to call out for help, but all I could do was thrash a little and moan. The nurse who had told me to stop flailing my arm hours before now told me to stop again. I tried to tell her that I couldn't breathe, but she didn't understand. I began spelling it in the air. "I can't breathe." But she didn't understand.

It got worse. Almost no air could reach my lungs now, and I tried to suck, but nothing happened. I tried to blow, but only a little air escaped. Panic was overcoming me, and I thrashed harder.

"Quit moving, RaNelle. Lie still," she said. "Try to relax."

Relax? I was dying! "It's clogged! It's clogged!" I tried to scream.

"You're just making things worse, RaNelle. Now lie still!"

I wanted to hit her, strangle her, but I couldn't even see her.

Snorting and sucking sounds were coming from my throat, but she couldn't hear them. After telling me to be quiet again, the nurse left.

I lay in agony for nearly an hour, giving all my energy to sucking in each breath. Gradually the gurgling sound got louder, and another nurse came in—the one I had been spelling to in the night. I felt her presence and began thrashing again.

"What's the matter?" she asked.

I spelled, "I can't breathe."

I felt the tube move and knew that she was looking at it. Then I felt searing pain as she pulled it part way out.

"Oh, my gosh," she said. "There's all kinds of junk down there. I'll be right back." She got an aspirator and inserted it down the tube, sucking up a large pool of gooey fluid. Phlegm from my throat had oozed into the opening at the bottom of the tube, almost completely blocking it. When she put the tube back, I could breathe. I took several large breaths then relaxed in relief.

The tube clogged again from time to time, and this same angelic nurse was always the one who fixed it. I couldn't communicate with anybody else.

For the next three days the doctors continued to slice my hands and let the fluids drain off into plastic bags, just as my grandmother had showed me. Each arm was positioned so my hands hung below the bed, letting the fluids run out of the incisions.

It wasn't until three days later that I was ready for the whirlpool. And even then, if I had known what they were going to do, I would never have accepted it. Although the pain from the burns was still incredibly intense, the rest of my body was feeling a little better, and I was looking forward to getting the mud and blood and dirt off me. I had been in an airplane accident less than seventy-two hours earlier and had walked down a mountain, and as far as I was concerned a bath would be just the right thing. The nurses laid me on a flat gurney and raised the whole unit over a tub of warm water. I could feel the steam rising up, slithering over my body. Then the realization hit me. Wait a minute, I thought. Hot water and burns don't mix. "No!" I tried to scream, but it was too late. They lowered me into the water, and I thought this time I *would* die.

People grabbed my arms and legs, and I felt something bite into my leg. Hard. I tried to scream as loudly as I could, but could only grunt through the tube. I tried to break free, but was held by strong hands, my head only inches out of the water. The hot water stung like alcohol. Something bit deeply into me again, and I screamed—a little more success-fully this time. Then I realized that the people had brushes and were scrubbing my wounds. Plastic bristles dug into my burns, tearing out dead skin and flesh from my arms, legs, hands, neck, and feet. I writhed to get free of the biting, tearing brushes, but I was held more firmly. I managed to force one eye open and I saw a chunk of flesh floating in red water. The whirlpool was filled with streaks of red and chunks of bloody refuse. The scrubbing continued until I thought I would pass out from the pain. I tried harder to break loose, but I was trapped, held down by too many peo-ple. Even as panic took over and made me scream louder and fight harder, I still couldn't get free. Every time I tried to scream I felt the tube in my throat grating on the burned membrane, but the screams were involuntary. I couldn't stop. Now the pain in my throat was nearly as great as the pain of the scrubbing, but my throat suffered with the rest of me.

That first session in the whirlpool seemed to last hours, but was actually only thirty minutes. I was to endure these scrubbings twice daily for weeks. They had to clean the dead tissue out of the wounds, but I thought, what good does cleaning the wounds do if it kills me in the process? I was virtually lifeless when they carried me back to my bed.

Later that afternoon as I lay on the bed I heard screams coming from the hallway—hideous, unendurable wails of agony. I wanted to stop my ears. I wanted to run from the awful torment, but I couldn't move. A nurse came in, and by motioning and grunting I managed to ask her about the screams.

"That's the whirlpool," she said. "That's where you were a while ago."

At least the other patients couldn't hear my screams, I thought. I couldn't even whimper. But hearing their screams made me relive my own trauma in the whirlpool, and I waited, anticipating the awful moment when the nurse would come and take me into that place again.

Days went by, and I lived from scrubbing to scrubbing, from screaming to screaming. Through it all I hadn't thought much about Terry because I had been so busy just trying to survive. The nurses had told me that he was okay in a room nearby recovering from his own wounds. But I knew his injuries were not as bad as mine, and now I began to wonder about him. With the pain from my burns mushrooming from pulse to pulse, crescendoing in a constant rhythm of anguish, I tried to remember when I had last heard his voice. Why hadn't he been in to see me? Where was he now? I lay like a fallen statue on the bed, staring at the dimpled ceiling, but the ceiling held no answers. For the next few days I lay between treatments, unmoving, unblinking, and wondering a thousand times, where is Terry? Where is my husband?

The nurses brought lights in—large, round, and orange— and positioned them around my body. They turned the lights on, and I heard an electrical sound, almost a crackling sound, and my mind went back to the burning plane. The lights instantly got hot, and I thought I could feel the flames again racing across my body. Before I knew it I was screaming for Terry to get out of the plane.

"Relax, RaNelle," a nurse's voice said. "This isn't the plane. These lamps will keep you warm so you don't go into hypothermia. Now stop screaming and let the lamps do their work."

The lamps went off for a time, but then came back on. I again saw the plane and felt the burns and screamed again for Terry.

The lamps went off. Then they came on again, and I felt the burns and screamed. And they went off.

This went on for three days—the scrubbings in the whirlpool, the lamps going on and off.

And Terry never came, and my tube plugged up again, and the scrubbings continued, and I came back lifeless to the bed.

"God," I asked to the dimpled ceiling that never moved, "if you wanted Terry and me to be together, where is he? If you spared him to help me, why isn't he here?" And one day I got the pad and wrote to my nurse, "Where is Terry?" And she said, "Ranelle, I don't know." But I felt she did know. Why wouldn't she talk to me? What was she avoiding? Or was it Terry who was avoiding me? I couldn't understand, but I knew I needed Terry then like I had never needed him before.

Chapter

T   E   N

TWO WEEKS LATER THEY TOOK THE TUBE OUT OF MY throat, and I was ready to start asserting myself. That morning in the whirlpool room when the nurses laid me in the water I began screaming and fighting like a tiger. My voice was raspy, but I could get a bigger breath now and could yell louder and fight harder. A young nurse tried to grab my leg, and I kicked her in the shoulder. She shot backwards like she'd been fired out of a cannon. Too late I saw that she was pregnant. Another nurse grabbed my arm. Whap! She got a mouthful of knuckles. I was crazy. They were *not* going to inflict pain on me again. I'd been through enough. I was in my anger. A young man held my head while the others scrambled for position. I turned and got his thumb between my teeth and chomped. He let out a screech that brought the rest of the staff in to assist—reinforcements that I quickly and easily dispatched. I would not be toyed with. I would not be tortured or flagellated or humiliated by people with brushes and foul intentions. I would fight back. Yes, I was in my anger now and could get oxygen, and I would vanquish an army of nurses and doctors if necessary. This whirlpool was mine.

The young man was stubborn, though, and grabbed my face again. But I had the move down and caught his index finger in my incisors and bit like I meant it. He would learn to leave me alone or forever hold his four-fingered hand. His face looked up at the sky, and he yelled like Hercules must have when the world landed on his shoulders. Other tenacious hands clawed at my arms again, and I spat his finger out, which unfortunately, was still connected to his hand, and did battle with the new aggressors. The young man stopped them with a command and came around so I could see him. It was Andy Sneibly, a physical therapist who specialized in burn care. He was the only one who scrubbed my face because it took the kind of precise and delicate work that he did best.

"I've had it," he said, and laid the brush down. Reaching over the rim of the metal tub, he took my face in his hands, and something told me not to fight.

"You and I are going to come to terms right now," he said, bringing my face close to his. "Stop fighting, do you understand? Quit this, now!"

"Do you want to trade places?" I asked.

"RaNelle," he said through clenched teeth, "you've got to quit this and get with the program. Do you understand?"

"I understand the program," I said, "and it's going to change."

It was great to be able to talk again.

"No, RaNelle, it isn't going to change. And I don't want any more of your temper tantrums. We can't work when you behave this way. You think you're the only one who's suffered like this? Let me tell you about somebody who's suffered more than you can even imagine. I love him more than you can understand. He walked the earth two thousand years ago and suffered so much in spirit that he sweat blood. That, RaNelle, is pain. It happens now and again; somebody bleeds from their pores. If you think it hurts when I scrub your face, imagine bleeding from every square inch of your body. And he said he did it for you. He sweat blood, RaNelle. The next time you think you're in pain, I want you to remember that."

Tears rolled down Andy's face, and I felt tears welling in my own eyes.

"He did it out of love," Andy continued, "and believe it or not, some of us are doing *this* out of love. We could be just about anywhere else. We don't need to be in the burn unit, but we choose to help those who need us most. I know the scrubbing hurts, but you've got to let us help you."

My own tears ran into my burns and stung, but I didn't care. I felt humbled. My grandmother had shown me the suffering Andy was talking about. She had shown me the horrendous pain of the darkest moment on earth, and my spirit had grieved as the sacrifice was made. It was a sacrifice of blood, just as Andy had said, and I agonized over falling short of that sacrifice. How could I have forgotten so easily? How could I have forgotten what I learned from my grandmother? She had shown me dignity and nobility and had filled me with a desire for these attributes, yet dignity and nobility had no place in me. *Oh, God,* I thought, *how could I fall so far so quickly? How could I so soon forget?* And I made a silent, solemn commitment right then that I would not scream or lash out again while in therapy.

They were about to hold me down and start scrubbing again, but I said no.

"Let me do it."

They looked at Andy. "What, RaNelle?" he asked.

"Give me the brush and let me scrub myself."

Quietly Andy gave me his brush. I started working it on my thigh. Up and down, up and down, I let the bristles flow across the ragged flesh and exposed muscle.

"Harder, RaNelle," one of the nurses said. "See that yellow stuff? You've got to get it out." And I brushed harder and felt the pain as the bristles dug in. But I didn't yell.

In and out I scrubbed, going deeper and deeper. I looked down and saw in horror that my thigh had opened up like a crater. Flayed, white flesh clung to my leg, dancing in the currents. My blood oozed out and turned the water brown. I thought I would be sick.

"Good, RaNelle, you've got it all," the nurse said. "Work on your hand now."

I breathed deeply and tried to prepare for the pain. Nausea swept over me as I scrubbed my left hand and wrist, but I kept at it until the wounds were clean. I worked for the next hour scrubbing every wound I could reach, following the nurses' directions, fighting the pain and sickness.

From that day on, I didn't scream or fight again. I may not have been dignified or noble like my grandmother, but I tried to suffer more silently. If I couldn't be full of love, I could at least be strong, or perhaps, sometimes, even gracious.

After each scrubbing, the pain resonated in me for hours. Ever grateful that I hadn't been burned on my back, I would lay absolutely still and stare at the ceiling above. Each square of tile there had hundreds of holes, maybe a thousand or more. Often, I started at the upper left and began counting but was soon lost in the pain. I needed something more taxing. So I began counting down from a thousand.

One thousand, nine hundred ninety-nine, nine hundred ninety-eight. . .

Several times I got into the seven hundreds before the pain made me shut my eyes. When that happened I would lie still, often hearing the muffled cries of someone in the whirlpool, and I would think about my children and Terry.

My children were still at my parents' home, and I didn't know how things were going there. I imagined the hardship on everyone, especially the children, but my parents had kindly not informed me of it. They came to visit me a week after the accident. The doctors thought I might be ready for my first surgery and had just performed the first skin graft. My mother promised to be there after I came out of the operating room.

In this first surgery, the doctors had used a tool that reminded me of a wood planer—a sharp blade that shaved off several inches of skin on my back. They said it skimmed off only the top layers of epidermis, but I was to find out later that this causes pain almost greater than the burns themselves. After removing the strip of skin, they pressed it in a machine that spread the skin to cover double the area it had come from. Then they sewed seams in it to custom fit it to my hand. The surgery had taken a couple of hours, and when I got back to my room I was growing weak.

I was still in intensive care, so the nurses hooked me up to the monitors. True to her word, my mother was there in a chair next to my bed. But as I lay near her, I felt my body shutting down, and I could hardly tell her how grateful I was that she had come. The surgery had been harder on me than they expected. I barely formed the words: "I think I'm dying, Mom."

"RaNelle, hold on." Her voice was panicked. "I'll get the nurse." She ran out of the room and I felt myself slipping, my breath and life getting fainter.

"Her signs are lower," the nurse said when they came back, "but they seem to have stabilized. Let's watch awhile and see if they come back up." My mother moved closer saying, "Hold on, honey."

"Mother, I'm leaving," I said.

"No, RaNelle, you're still here. Fight it, honey."

"I can see things. Grandma's here again. Her hand is on mine. Put your hand on top of Grandma's."

My mother's eyes filled with tears at the thought of her own mother's presence. She placed her hand on mine, and I saw it resting inside my grandmother's translucent hand.

For the next two hours I fought between life and death, my mother and grandmother both encouraging me to live. It is through sheer will, I found out, that we can accomplish great things. I have no doubt that divine help was given me, but I could have refused it and gone on to the other side. I had to accept it, to fight for it, to become a part of the divine will itself. Then my flesh responded to the will of the spirit, and I lived.

I reflected on the precious gift of life that my mother and grandmother had helped me to keep. I could still be a mother again to my children. I could still be a wife, I thought. But where was my husband? Where had Terry gone? I had been told by one of the nurses that he was still in the hospital, but not in intensive care. She said he was working through things.

One day I thought I heard his voice outside my room.

"Terry!" I called out.

He appeared in the doorway with a nurse who was taking him to another area for therapy. His hands were bandaged. "I'm in a hurry, I can't stay," he said. "I've got to go." And he left.

I sat in a kind of shock for hours. Who was this man? Was he still my husband? Were we still supposed to be together?

One night the windows lit up during a terrible thunderstorm, and I found myself beating at the flames again, and yelling at Terry to get out of the plane, crying that he was burning up, that I was burning up. A male nurse came in and held me.

"You're not in the plane," he said, calming me. "You're here with us, in the hospital." The storm lasted all night, and he stayed with me, speaking gently after each flash, keeping me from going back to the plane. Why wasn't it Terry who was here with me?

One day my grandfather, my mother's father, came to visit. He had suffered seven strokes and had no business leaving the house, but when he heard that my grandmother, his wife, had met me when I died, he insisted that a grandson put him in the car and drive him from Tremonton, near the Utah-Idaho border, to Salt Lake City.

He fairly bounded into my room—despite his frailty—grinning and vibrant. In my raspy voice I told him how good he looked. He smiled, artfully choosing not to say how bad I looked. Instead, he said, "You have something important to tell me."

"Yes, how do you know?"

"I just know."

"Grandpa, something wonderful has happened, but I don't know how to tell you about it." I was concerned about shocking him too much, possibly causing another stroke. "I saw Grandma," I said tentatively.

"I know," he said. "Please tell me what she said."

Picking my words carefully, I told him of my visit to the other side. Then I described Grandma, young, twenty-five, giggly. He was absolutely still. I shared truths she had taught me, the love of God, the work done there, the work we should do here, helping and serving others. Then came messages that

my grandmother had told me to take back to him but which I
had forgotten until the moment they left my mouth. It was as
she had said; I was remembering things as they were needed.
Grandpa had come, exercising his faith to hear these words,
and they came for him. When I finished, he was in tears, his
face shining. I could remember nothing of what I had said. It
was as before; the words were buried, never to come to my
recollection again. My grandfather seemed transformed.

"RaNelle," he said. "You'll never hear me say this again,
but I love you." He sat in silence, tears still trickling down his
face.

I was stunned. Why wouldn't he say it again? Was it his
pride? I couldn't remember him ever saying he loved me
before, and now the words felt so good I could almost taste
them. I wanted to say, "No, Grandpa, tell me again. Let the
words be music to both of us." But he got up and left, walking out the door with my cousin.

Two days later, I felt that something was wrong. A tremendous loneliness settled upon me, a melancholy that made me
ache and weep. I had learned that Terry had been moved into
the room next to me, but I didn't feel that this was the only
cause for my grief—the fact that he was so near but didn't
visit. Something else was wrong. Something important was
missing. The nurses were uneasy around me. I asked one or
two what had happened, and they said that nothing had happened. I wept through the day and night, desolate. The next
morning I finally got a nurse to talk to me.

"I know something is wrong," I said. "What is it?"

The nurse pursed her lips, fighting inside. "I'm not supposed to tell you. Your mother is coming. She'll tell you."

"Please," I said. "I can feel it—something's terribly wrong.
I won't let you go until you tell me."

"Your grandfather died yesterday," she said. "He had another stroke. We weren't supposed to tell you because we thought it might upset you."

"Thank you," I said. "Thank you for telling me."

She left the room, and I quickly put it all together. The cause of my sudden loneliness became clear. My grandmother was gone.

I realized now that she had been with me constantly since my return. She had strengthened me with her presence after my surgery. She had sustained me in moments when I wanted to die. She had encouraged me, and without knowing it, I had been feeling her ceaseless love. She was away from me now. She was with my grandfather.

Now my grandfather's last words made sense. He had known about my message for him. He had been given strength to come and hear it, and I had been given sudden recollection to share it. Then he had left to prepare, using the brief time only he knew he had. And two days later he was reunited with Grandma. He had used his last chance to tell me he loved me. I would never hear him say that again—not in this life.

I cried through much of the day, lamenting my misunderstanding, weeping for the loss of my grandmother and because I had not known until then that she had been constantly with me. My loneliness was palpable. Oh, Grandma and Grandpa, I wanted to say, I love you both! Please don't leave me again. But the desolation remained, and over the next few hours I became inconsolable.

Then Terry was by my side.

"I heard about your grandfather," he said. "I'm sorry." He found a stool by the wall and brought it over. "Is there anything I can do?"

"No. I just miss them."

"Them?"

"Grandma. She'd been here with me until Grandpa died."

Terry said nothing.

"I miss them, Terry. I miss them because they were here. I miss them because they comforted me and strengthened me. They were here, Terry. But do you know what I wonder?" He shook his head. "I wonder where you were."

"RaNelle, I came in to see you," he said softly.

"No you didn't. I never saw you. You went by the door once, and I called out to you, but you couldn't even come in for a second. You were too busy to see me."

"I *was* busy, RaNelle. They've had me in therapy almost ten hours a day. But I did come in. I came in and lay down next to you twice, and I got in trouble and they said they'd move me if I did it again."

I looked at him in disbelief. "You came in and lay down on my bed?"

"Yes, but I got caught."

"I don't believe it. I would've woken up."

"I thought you would have too, but you didn't."

"No, Terry, what about when I was awake? What about the mornings before your therapy? What about dinner time? At least you can eat. I've still got this I.V. hooked up to me. Couldn't you come be with me a moment? Couldn't you say hi?"

"I tried, RaNelle. But you don't know how hard . . ." His voice trailed off.

"What? How hard what is? Look at me. How hard what is?"

"I'm sorry."

"I know."

"RaNelle, I tried. You don't know how hard it is . . ."

"What is?"

"It's my fault this . . . happened. I'm sorry."

"You're sorry? Then why didn't you come . . ."

"I'd better go. This wasn't a good idea." He got off his stool and quickly left the room.

I cried again, grieving from the deepest part of me that someone I loved had left me.

And through the wall I heard him crying.

"Oh, God," I thought, "what has happened to us?"

As the room dimmed with evening, the loneliness and melancholy thickened. I missed Grandma more than ever. And I missed Grandpa too, wanting to hear him say I love you again. But now, all my tears spent, in a strange way I missed Terry. Not like before. Not in anger. I let my hand gently touch the surface of the sheet next to me, feeling its soft folds. Had he truly been here?

I looked up at the ceiling and saw the holes, and I began to count.

Chapter

E L E V E N

TERRY LEFT THE HOSPITAL SEVERAL DAYS LATER. IT HAD been three weeks now since the accident. I was wheeled into his room and spoke to him before he left. His therapy had gone well, and he had begun to use his hands, though they were scarred for life. He had lost his job, and the prospect of finding another job in his field—one that required using his hands with computers—was daunting. He didn't know if they'd work as they had before. We also now faced huge debts. Insurance had covered only the loss of the plane; we didn't have casualty insurance. The hospital bills were completely on our shoulders, and they were already into the hundreds of thousands of dollars. Those were real debts, obligations that we couldn't just check out of, like Terry checking out of the hospital. No matter how lucky he got with a job or how hard he worked, he would never be able to pay those bills back in his lifetime. The weight of this was like a rock on us both.

Terry would be caring for the kids by himself. They hadn't seen us in three weeks, and for Jason, who was just about to turn two, and Christina, almost four, it had been too long. My mother and sisters had cared for them wonderfully, but the children were feeling abandoned by their parents. Christina in particular couldn't understand what had happened to her mom and dad or why she couldn't go home. Terry had always been a loving father, but with his hands still in bandages, he wasn't sure about meals and changing diapers and getting the kids up and dressed. His face was still red from the burns, and he wondered if the children would even recognize him. Life would not be the same, and he was facing it alone.

We didn't kiss good-bye; I had no lips, and I could see that my appearance still shocked him. The doctors had put eighty staples in my face to hold my skin grafts together. Perhaps seeing me this way intensified his feelings of guilt. In any event, divorce was not brought up. We were literally in no shape to leave each other.

Terry left the hospital and I stayed behind. Not much had changed really; I was alone in my room and Terry was somewhere else.

Now that Terry had taken the children home to Bakersfield, my mother flew in every other week . Her visits lessened my loneliness, but the stress of therapy and the slowness of recovery at times made me despondent. Although I hadn't seen my face—mirrors are strategically nonexistent in the burn unit—I remembered the gruesome sight in the sheriff's mirror. I had been hideous, terrifying, and I considered the prospect of looking like a freak the rest of my life. My dreams for a career were shattered. I would never have a normal life—do the things normal people do. How would I manage? How could I live like this? My mother noticed I was sinking into despair.

Then one day a cousin of mine showed up, Peter Jeppson. He was a popular speaker around the country. Peter had been severely burned in a car accident and had found success in life despite the scars on his face and body. Thousands came to hear him speak at motivational seminars. I knew that my mother had sent him. I was not in the mood to be cheered up just then, so when he asked me how I was, I gave him an overdose of grief and self-pity.

I didn't get even halfway through when he stopped me and said, "Look RaNelle. I can see you don't really want to hear what I have to say, so I'll be brief; then you'll never have to see me again. First, you need to read a book called *As A Man Thinketh*. And second, you can do anything you want, RaNelle. It's all in your mind. The scars are meaningless. The handicaps are nothing. What matters is that you believe in yourself. That's it. That's all. Good-bye." He left.

I was surprised by the sudden pronouncement and his even more sudden departure. True to his word, he never showed up again, but his words wouldn't leave. Maybe it *was* all in my mind. Maybe I *could* do things—normal things—if I wanted. After all, I had decided not to scream again in the whirlpool, and I hadn't. It fit what my grandmother had said about the power of our thoughts. We are what we think. Maybe my mind was strong enough to make things happen. Maybe I could live a semi-normal life again.

But one of the doctors put an end to that kind of thinking when the final diagnosis came back on my internal injuries. My body had suffered a lot of damage from the accident and from the trauma of the fire. But the worst news was what he told my mother: "Your daughter will probably never be able to have another child. The body's immune system will begin to attack itself, and although I can't be sure it will happen this time, the reproductive organs are often the first to go."

I was devastated. What about Nathaniel? He had called me Mom. Could Nathaniel and my grandmother be mistaken? What should I make of this? A positive mental attitude would have to go a long way.

And that's when Whitey came along.

They had just moved me from the isolation of intensive care to a room with a view of almost the whole burn unit. Whitey was the first person I saw in the rehabilitation unit outside my door. He was a farmer from Idaho who had tried to stop a range fire on his ranch. The flames had circled back to trap him, and the heat had been so intense that even the handle of his shovel had been reduced to charcoal. He was burned over ninety percent of his body and had already been in the burn unit for several months. He looked like scars on a skeleton. Every part of his body that was visible was nothing but stretched and browned scar tissue. From my bed I watched the nurses strap him on a tilt table.

Because he had been off his feet so long, the tendons in his legs had shortened and pulled his heels back, making his feet point down. Once Whitey was strapped in, the nurses tilted the table down so his feet, which were hanging over the side, could reach the floor. He was supposed to put as much weight on his feet as possible to begin stretching the tendons back into place. The table was rigged so that he could even walk a few steps. But the pain was enormous, both from still-healing scars and from the unused tendons being stretched, and he immediately pulled his feet up.

"You've got to do it, Whitey," the nurses said. "You've got to work those legs, get those muscles flexing again."

Tentatively, he placed his feet on the floor again and tried to bear some weight. He couldn't do it. Again he tried, but the pain was too much.

"Come on, Whitey," one of the nurses said. "Get those feet on the floor and work your legs."

He tried again and jerked back in pain.

"Try to walk," another nurse said. "Get those feet moving."

And he tried again, and couldn't do it. And when they told him to do it again and again, he started crying.

The discouragement showed in agony on his face, creating an almost absurd and unreal sight. He was bald—as were all the patients in the burn unit to limit possible breeding areas for bacteria—and his deformed face streaming with glistening tears looked like a special effect from a movie set. He began pounding the table with his fists and the nurses yelled at him to stop.

"That's not constructive!" they'd yell. "Knock it off! Start moving your legs." And Whitey's head went limp over one shoulder and tears ran down his arm as he sobbed.

I began crying for him, wanting to get out of bed and help him through the exercise, but there was nothing I could do. I watched him work through that terrible ordeal for two hours, not once taking a step or putting weight on his foot for more than a second or two. When they removed him from the table I felt like I had just previewed the agonies of hell.

The next day Whitey was placed on the table and went through the whole ordeal again. I was in tears again when he was done, my stomach churning, my mind searching for some way to help him. This was crazy, I thought. He's gone through ten times the suffering I have. What was I doing complaining, feeling sorry for myself? A few days later Whitey put some pressure on his toes and held it there. He cried but he wouldn't pull his feet back. It was sheer will, blatant determination. I wept again and committed myself to help him any way I could. A few days later, they told him to try to hold his weight up without the table, to hang on to a rail and walk. He began to fall and they caught him. This went on for another two hours, without him taking a single step away from the rail.

I was going through my own therapy now and was allowed out of bed. My ankles and legs were still healing from the burns, but I was allowed to hobble about to keep my muscles and tendons from atrophying. Most of my therapy involved my hands and fingers, relearning simple motions and dexterity. One of my nurses saw how much I was struggling with therapy, and she began bringing Jelly Bellies into my room at night.

"If you can pick these up with your fingers," she said, "I'll let you eat them." Our diets were strictly regulated, allowing no candy, so this was a real treat. She spread them out on the table across my bed, and I tried to pick one up and realized immediately how difficult this was going to be. But I worked at it. She came in nightly for a week or so, until I could successfully pick up every jelly bean. This motivation and care really made a difference in my spirits and eventual dexterity.

A few days later when Whitey was brought out and placed by the rail, I left my bed—pulling my I.V. bottle along behind me—and limped out to him. The nurses were surprised.

"Let me help him," I said. "We'll walk together."

Whitey seemed willing, and the nurses finally gave in, although they weren't sure that I could walk yet myself. I put my arm around his waist and helped him take a step. His I.V. was on a rack on one side, and mine was on the other. He held my shoulder and leaned on me. "That's right," I said, "just hold me and bring your feet around." Two of his toes wouldn't straighten; the tendons had curled them under his feet, and he had to drag them. "Try to get it a little higher," I said, encouraging him to lift his leg high enough to clear his toes from the floor. "That's it. One more step. Come on." And gradually we walked to the other side of the room.

As we hobbled and clung to each other, our bottles clattering behind us, dignity and decorum were thrown out. Our gowns, which tied in back, fell open as we struggled together, presenting quite a view, no doubt, to the nurses and therapists behind us—probably not a view they wanted to repeat. But we turned and came back the other way, our gowns almost totally gone now, and eventually we made it back to the rail. Whitey was exhausted but beaming as he nodded his head; he couldn't speak yet. I was exhausted and just wanted to get back to bed. But we had more work to do. We got our robes straight and made another trip across the room and back. Eventually we got to where we could recognize each other more from backsides than from our bandaged faces.

Only a burn victim knows the pain that comes from getting out of bed and standing up during the first few weeks of therapy. The blood immediately flows to your wounds, creating a pounding pain that rivals the fire itself. The doctors had layered me in anti-fungal cream and wrapped me in yards of flesh-colored mesh called Coban. Then they wrapped ace bandages around the Coban until I looked like a mummy. This gave support to the burns so they didn't bleed, but it turned simple activities like walking and eating into monumental challenges. Also, every two hours a new sterile solution called TAB, or Triple Antibiotic, had to be injected under the wrap to kill the common forms of bacteria that float in the air. It was not fun, but I was more than willing to go through the pain of standing and the discomfort of walking to help Whitey. He was worth anything to me. I loved Whitey. Not only because he had taken me out of my own misery and self-pity, but because he was a good and fun-loving person. I enjoyed sacrificing for him.

Whitey looked like a skeleton because he couldn't keep his weight up. He was being fed twenty-four hours a day through his tube and was also being forced to eat three meals a day, but he couldn't keep any flesh on his bones. That was because burn victims devour calories. Being hypermetabolic, they can burn more than twice their normal intake of calories. A burn victim's resting pulse rate is somewhere around 150, and their respiratory rate is twice that of normal. Whitey needed help gaining weight. One day during therapy, I came up with a plan to help him.

The nurses had a hard time getting me to use my fingers in therapy because they hurt so much. Every time I bent a finger, the scars would crack or bunch up and the tendons would burn. I hated the exercises. But then I came up with my plan. If the therapist would give me a nickel per exercise, I would do each one over and over. I bribed these good people out of all their change daily, and, I am glad to say, Whitey was soon the better for it.

I stored the money in my bed. Whenever my mother came, I would ask her for a quarter or two. She couldn't figure out why I needed it since I couldn't go anywhere, but she usually relented and gave me something. Finally I had enough money to set my plan in motion.

One night when all the nurses were gone except the one watching the monitors, I slipped out of bed and gathered my coins as quietly as I could. I sneaked out past the nurse, through the burn unit, down the hall towards the main doors leading to the rest of the hospital. Just then I heard a man's voice coming from behind me. Uh oh, I thought, a doctor—I'm in trouble now. Burn patients were confined to their own area of the building. Who knew what dangerous bacteria lurked in other parts of the hospital? It was a rule strictly enforced. Also, I wasn't supposed to be out of bed, and, worse than that, I was as naked as a baby; patients in the burn unit slept without robes. Actually, I was not that naked. I had wraps on my arms and legs, but they didn't cover the vital areas. I would be in real trouble if anybody saw me, and, probably, so would they. The voice was coming closer. I rushed to a closet door and tried to open it, but it was locked, and I became frantic. I limped over to another door across the hall and yanked. It opened, much to my relief, and I went in. It was the doctors' lounge, and I quickly scanned the room for something to wear, but found nothing. I heard a noise and my heart jumped. I turned around and saw the handle moving. The doctor was coming in. I looked around and saw another door, and I darted through it. It was the bathroom.

"Hee, hee," came a high-pitched voice. "Hee, hee, hee."

Oh great, I thought. He's got a nurse with him, and they're going to do it right here in the lounge.

"Hee, hee," she giggled again.

I had left the bathroom door slightly open for light, and I jumped into a shower against the opposite wall and pulled the curtain shut. Then I looked down and noticed that the curtain didn't reach the floor, and I realized that if one of them came in, they'd see my feet for sure. I breathed deeply.

So did the doctor.

"Hee, hee," I heard again.

"Don't freak, RaNelle," I said to myself. "Stay calm."

The doctor and nurse had remained in the lounge area, and the doctor was putting a move on the nurse, saying something about love and pent-up passion, and suddenly I recognized his voice. It wasn't the doctor at all; it was one of the male nurses. The woman said something in return, her voice breathless, and I tried to place her voice too, but I couldn't. I didn't think they were making love, but it was obvious that things were getting heated. Great, I thought, I don't want to listen to this, and I poked my head through the curtain to look for another way out. The woman said something about making love, and the guy started panting. He was panting louder than I ever heard anybody pant before. She giggled. He panted again, incredibly loud.

It must have scared her.

"Okay, come on," she said, "stop that."

His panting was ferocious now.

"Really," she said, "I've got to get back on duty. Let's get out of here. Hey, stop that!"

I'll never know what it was he had to stop.

"Come on," she said, "get serious. Quit it. I've really got to get back."

To my utter relief, she won the tug-of-war, and they left the room. As soon as the door shut behind them, I was out of the shower looking for another exit. There wasn't one, so I waited a minute then went back to the lounge door and poked my head out.

I saw another door nearby leading to the whirlpool, and I slipped over and looked inside.

Jackpot. A lab coat hung from a rack just inside the door. I went inside and put it on, buttoning it as high as it would go. I wrapped a towel around my head, covering as much of my face and forehead as I could, and tucked the ends of it under the collar of the coat. I hoped I looked like I had just come out of the shower and was in a hurry to get somewhere—all of which was true. I grabbed an extra towel and left the room.

Newly emboldened, I went forward with the plan, walking through the main doors leading to the rest of the hospital. I put the extra towel in the door so it wouldn't close, but if somebody came through that door and moved the towel before I came back, it would lock me out, and I'd have to ring the buzzer to get back in. Then there'd be real trouble. I moved quickly to the elevator and pushed the button. It opened, and, gratefully, I found it was empty. I stepped in and pushed the button for the lobby. The elevator started but slowed just a few floors down. My heart stopped. The doors opened and a doctor stepped in.

I turned away and acted as if I were studying my feet. The elevator closed and proceeded down. I could almost read his thoughts.

"May I help you?" he finally asked.

This was it. "Uh, yes," I said, still fascinated with my feet. "Could you tell me where the gift shop is?"

"It's on the main floor." He paused, still eyeing me, knowing that the button for the main floor was already lit up. "Is there anything else I can do for you?"

"No, uh, thank you. I'm fine."

I heard his feet shuffle as he tried to get a look at my face.

I tried to act nonchalant and turned farther away from him. The elevator finally stopped and the doors opened. He didn't say anything as I rushed out in my awkward limp and walked past the reception desk. It was closed for the night, but the gift shop was still open—incredibly good luck. I went inside, holding all of my change in my hand—all the coins I had bribed and begged from people—and I went to the candy counter. A rush hit my head as I saw Snickers and Reeses and Milky Ways and a host of other forbidden fare. It seemed like it had been forever since I had eaten chocolate. Then I saw my favorite treat, Ice Cubes! And I scooped up a handful in my bandaged hand. I'd loved Ice Cubes since I was a kid, squares of creamy chocolate individually wrapped and delicately cared for. They were works of culinary art. I put the whole handful on the counter and said, "Give me as many of these as I can pay for," and I laid the money down beside them. My towel was pulled about as far over my forehead and cheeks as I could possibly manage and still be able to see.

"Will that be it, ma'am?" the clerk asked when she was through counting. I lifted my head a little and said, "Yes, thank you very much."

Our eyes met, and hers suddenly grew wide. "Oh, my!" she exclaimed raising her hands to her face and stepping back. She took a couple of deep breaths then composed herself. "I'm sorry," she said. "I didn't mean to do that. Really, I'm sorry."

I laughed for the first time in a long time. "Never mind," I said. "Don't worry about it. Can you put these in a bag for me?"

"Oh, yes. Here." She took the candies and put them all in a nice little white bag. "Thank you for coming," she said.

It was almost time for the nurses' nightly rounds; I would have to hurry. I went back to the elevator and went up to my floor. I got back to the main doors and saw the towel still there. Luck was with me tonight. I was almost home! I slipped in and went straight to my room, walking past the nurse who was now half sprawled on the desk and cutting z's like a chain saw. I took off my new coat, threw it under my bed, and tucked myself and the candy under the covers.

I almost chuckled in my cleverness.

Several minutes later a nurse approached the bed on her rounds.

"Hello, RaNelle. Where have you been tonight?" She stood above me with arms folded like a parent.

"What?" I said, trying to open my eyes. I was an expert at feigning grogginess.

"I came by earlier, and you weren't here."

"Uh, I was here," I said, trying to wake up.

"Oh, no you weren't. I even looked in the bathroom. Did you go to the bathroom?"

"Yes, a while ago, I went to the bathroom."

"No, you didn't. I would have seen you. Where were you?"

"I was in the bathroom. You must have just missed me."

"Missed you in the bathroom?"

"I was there, I told you."

"No, you weren't."

"I was too."

Her voice rose. "Tell me where you were!"

"I already did. I was in the bathroom." I looked her in the eye with my steely stare, daring her to call me a liar.

Her face finally broke into a smile. "All right," she said. "You know, and I know, that you weren't in the bathroom, but if you want me to believe you were, well, that's all right I guess. Just don't do it again." She left, and I waited until my heart stopped pounding, then I got up and put on my new lab coat and gathered up the candy. She had disappeared around the corner, and the other nurse was still asleep at the desk. I stole across the floor to Whitey's room.

"Whitey . . . " I whispered. His eyes blinked open. "I've got a surprise for you."

He still didn't have the strength to talk clearly, but his mouth dropped open when he saw the booty in my hands.

"It's the best chocolate you'll ever taste, Whitey. Do you want one?"

"Uh huh!" He tried to sit up, and I pulled his pillow under him. Then, sitting on the edge of his bed, I took one of the Ice Cubes and peeled off the thin foil. My therapist would have been proud.

"Okay, you've got to open real wide. Can you do that?"

"Uh huh!" And he opened his mouth as wide as the burns on his lips and cheeks would allow, and I put one Ice Cube on his tongue.

He chewed slowly then stopped, letting the chocolate melt in his mouth. Tears formed in his eyes, and he stared at me. It was the purest communication he could make.

"You're welcome, Whitey," I said, and I put most of the other chocolates under his sheet, keeping a few for myself.

"Now, you've got to keep these hidden. If they find them, they'll take them away and want to know how you got them. Okay?"

"Uh huh." He nodded.

"Okay." I watched him begin chewing again, little sucking sounds coming from his mouth.

"Whitey?" I said.

"Huh?" He stopped chewing.

"Thank you." We looked at each other in a moment of pure love. "I promise that I'll do whatever I can to help you. I've got to go now."

Back in my room, I found it hard to sleep. I was thinking of how happy Whitey was. Then I bit into one of the chocolates. And then I *knew* how happy he was.

I loved him, and I thanked him in my mind for his courage, his being there, his allowing me to help him. I also thanked God in prayer for giving me such a friend. I could forget myself because of him; in some ways I could do more for him than I could for myself, and he accepted it like a child. As I lay in bed buzzing with this love, I seemed to feel my grandmother nearby—not saying anything.

Just smiling.

IT'S INTERESTING HOW YOU CAN LIVE IN A PLACE AND NOT really see it until something brings it into focus. My attitude was changing, and my eyes were opening to the world outside my own pain. I awoke one morning and saw blue, tightly-woven carpet covering the entire floor of the burn unit, and I wondered why I hadn't noticed it before. I got out of bed, feeling the carpet for the first time through the damaged skin of my feet. I had become familiar with the ceiling of course, but only the part directly over my bed where I had counted holes for endless stretches of time. Now I saw that there were holes all over the ceiling, thousands of them, covering the suspended ceiling which lay over the room like a white lid. I noticed the color of the walls. White. Blue and white, non-threatening, from the cool side of the spectrum. Good colors for the burn unit. Making my way through the door, I noticed a Radio Flyer wagon and a pile of toys. I hadn't been to that side of the burn unit often and wondered about them. The answer hit me before I could ask.

I had heard small, high voices crying in the whirlpool room, and now as I made my way around the unit, pretending that I was walking for therapy, I saw children lying in intensive care beds and in other rooms. Some had mothers or other family with them. Some were alone. I walked by the whirlpool room and saw a doctor wrapping a little girl, no more than two, in Coban and pressure bandages. His manner was gentle and caring. The child was burned on her legs and buttocks. She cried with a weary voice, already fatigued from the incessant pain. I entered and asked what had happened to her.

"Abuse," the assisting nurse said. "She was punished for wetting her pants. Her mother put her in a bathtub of scalding water."

I gasped.

The nurse, however, was steeled against such tragedies and looked on with a clear, unblinking stare. The child lay limp on the table as the doctor applied the dressings and bandages. I asked how long the girl had been in the burn unit.

"A couple of hours," the nurse said. "People don't realize how sensitive a baby's skin is. Water that adults bathe in can burn a baby."

"What happened to the mother?"

"Charges are being filed and she'll go to jail—I hope. It's hard to know. We get this all the time. After awhile the babies leave, scarred for life. We never know what happens to the parents."

The doctor was finishing up and I left. The girl was still crying, her voice becoming weaker. Sheer fatigue will make her sleep tonight, I thought. Then I remembered the pain of my own burns only four weeks earlier. Fatigue *doesn't* stop the pain; you feel it in your sleep.

I walked into the main area and saw another child, a two-year-old boy. He was walking along the blue carpet with the help of his parents. Both legs were wrapped from hips to toes and his parents praised and encouraged him with each ginger step. I walked through the burn unit and saw that all thirteen

rooms were filled. A couple of doors from my own was a tod-
dler, lying on her back asleep. Her mother was sleeping in a
chair. The little girl's face was swollen and covered with burns
with red welts running from the hairline to the neck. A nurse
came in and checked the girl. It was Lezli, one of the nurses
who had spent a lot of time working with me.

"What happened, Lezli?" I asked.

"Kitchen accident," she said. "She pulled a pan of boiling
spaghetti on herself."

I watched in silence as Lezli checked the girl's wounds. The
burns on her shaved head still oozed fluids.

"Has she been here awhile?"

"About ten days. She's past the worst of it. She'll live."

"She'll live?" I asked. "You mean boiling water can kill a
child?"

"It depends on how young the child is and how bad the
burns are. It was real close with this one. She's lucky."

I looked at the burns again. She would be terribly disfigured,
physically and probably emotionally, the rest of her life. But
she was alive, and maybe her scars would make her strong.
Then I thought of my own scars. Would they make *me* strong?

My therapy that day consisted of laying my hands flat on a
table and tapping my fingers up and down. First my index
finger, then my third finger, then my ring finger, then my little finger. The scars were so stiff and my tendons were still so
tight from surgery and the burns that I could barely move
them. All my fingers wanted to do was curl under and be left
alone. I finally finished the therapy, though, and extracted
fifty cents from Robin, my therapist. Ice Cubes would be on
the menu again shortly.

The next morning I got up and walked the hallways again.
No longer did I have to guard against viewers from behind;

my mother had bought me a new robe, and I could wander the halls fearlessly now. I saw Lezli with the little girl who had spilled the spaghetti. The girl was awake, staring at the ceiling. Her mother was gone.

"How is she?" I asked. The girl was motionless, her eyes fixed on the ceiling.

"Coming along," Lezli said. "We need to get her to eat."

"Is she losing weight?"

"No, but she lost a lot of weight that first week." Lezli stepped into the hall and gazed across the large central room of the burn unit. I shuffled after her. "At least she'll make it," Lezli said. "We had a two-year-old come in yesterday who'd been scalded by her mother. We lost her."

"What?"

Lezli turned and looked at me, concern on her face.

"She died?" I asked.

Lezli touched my arm. "I'm sorry, RaNelle. Did you know her?"

"No, but I saw her yesterday when the doctor was bandaging her." Tears came to my eyes. "Lezli, I thought she would be all right. She looked like she would make it."

"Children are so sensitive," she said. "Their little bodies can't take much trauma. She died at about four this morning."

I went to my room to wait for the next session of therapy. Who was the lucky one, I wondered, the girl who had lived or the girl who had died? One lived and struggled in mortality, the other had moved on to that world of light and love.

Maybe they both were lucky.

I had no answers.

I thought again about how we can live with something for a long time and not see it. I had been in the burn unit for a month now and hadn't seen death until today. Yet it had haunted this place all along like an ever-present ghost. Lives ended here. Some doctors and nurses wouldn't volunteer for the burn unit. They considered it dirty work. Even celebrities giving charity went to every other part of the hospital to visit children, but they never came here. Our doors were locked. Was it to keep others out or us in? Misery found meaning in this place.

My eyes were opening. Like the child burned by spaghetti or the little girl who died from burns her mother inflicted, I would face a future uniquely my own. For good or ill, I knew that I would have to make my own fate.

I had begun to identify with this place. I had faced it and accepted it as a part of my life, my identity. But I hadn't really faced myself yet; I didn't even know how I looked.

What *did* I look like?

There were no mirrors in the burn unit, so I would need to find one. At the birth of one of my children, in another hospital, I had put on my makeup one day using a foil strip from a food tray. It had acted as a perfect little mirror. Suddenly I became anxious for dinner, knowing that I would see my face for the first time in a month. Finally they brought in my dinner, and in my impatience I had trouble getting the lid off the tray as my fingers fumbled and slipped. Using my elbows, I succeeded in taking it off, and I looked inside.

Those son-of-a-guns, I thought, *they took the mirror out.*

I was furious. I bet everybody else in the hospital got a foil strip in their trays, but not the burn patients. But I wasn't giving up. I would see what I looked like if it killed me. I threw my feet over the side of the bed and shuffled out of the room. Two male nurses saw me leave.

"Where are you going, RaNelle?" one of them said.

"To the bathroom."

They looked at each other in disbelief. I hadn't been using the bathroom because of my burns and wraps—a fact which surely hadn't escaped the nurse's mind the night she couldn't find me.

"Really, RaNelle," he asked, "to the bathroom?"

"Yes, really. Now help me."

They actually became excited. A patient wanting to use the bathroom was showing progress in rehabilitation.

There was no mirror in the patients' bathroom of course. I knew that. But I wasn't heading for that bathroom. I was heading for the nurses' bathroom. The two young men whispered behind me. "Wow, this is great. I didn't think she'd ever use it." And I kept shuffling toward the wrong bathroom like I knew what I was doing, which I did. In their excitement they must have forgotten why patients with facial disfiguration use the bathroom with no mirrors. One male nurse opened the door and waited for me to go in.

"Do you want to go in by yourself?" he asked.

"Yes, I'll be fine. Just leave me alone."

He closed the door behind me, and I saw a glint of light to my left. The mirror.

I looked away and took a deep breath. Then I turned to it to see myself.

The inhuman thing looking back at me had absolutely no resemblance to RaNelle Wallace. I screamed, then gasped for air and screamed again. The figure in the mirror screamed back, mimicking every movement.

My head was bald and scabbed, and my face was almost twice the size of normal, still bloated like a basketball. Reconstructive surgeries had not begun yet on my face, and raw flesh hung from where my nose used to be and from around my exposed teeth. The living tissue, brushed clean by the scrubbings, dangled in red and white clumps. Yellow eschar, the substance that forms scabs, rimmed the wounds and dripped down my face. Bloody, purple crust met my gums where my lips should have been. But perhaps most horrible of all, two short wires hung out of my nostrils above my teeth. One was a thin tube which was hooked up to a feeding tube during the day. The other was used to keep the first tube from clogging. Both went down into my stomach.

Still screaming, I put my face close to the mirror to see if I could find me. I wasn't there. The face belonged to some other creature. Then I saw the eyes. The *eyes*. *They* were *mine*. Oh no, I thought in horror, this is me.

Then I heard a voice that began to sing so clearly that I turned to see who had come in, but I was alone. It was a man's voice, and it sang a song from my Sunday school days, a song I had sung many times with my own children:

> I am a child of God,
> And He has sent me here,
> Has given me an earthly home
> With parents kind and dear.

A feeling of peace came over me and I began to cry. I knew what was happening because of the warmness in my heart and the gentleness of the voice, but I didn't want to feel this right now. I didn't want this gentle burning. I wanted to feel the horror and rejection of my own face. I wanted to feel the pain it would give me the rest of my life. But the song, in this beautiful male voice, increased in intensity:

> Lead me, guide me, walk beside me,
> Help me find the way.
> Teach me all that I must do
> To live with Him someday.

The power of these final words softened me, taking out all the fight, and I fell to the floor, crying. The door opened.

The nurse who had opened the door for me rushed in. "What happened?" he asked. Other nurses came in and tried to pick me up. "Are you okay?" they said. "What happened?" I was holding my face, and one of them saw the mirror.

"Oh, RaNelle," she said.

Then the others saw, but they misunderstood. I was crying, but not for my face; I was crying because the song had begun again and it echoed through my whole being.

"Oh, I'm sorry," the young man said. "I'm so sorry." He and the others picked me up. "RaNelle, please . . . I'm so sorry."

They took me to my bed and laid me down, but I couldn't stop crying. The song repeated again and again through me, loud and clear. An hour and a half later I was still hearing it.

The male nurse came in again. He was crushed by what had happened.

"RaNelle," he said. "What can I do to help you? Is there anything at all? Please, let me help you."

I tried to hold back the sobs for a moment, but the words, "Lead me, guide me, walk beside me," came again, and I was reduced to uncontrollable tears.

"Is it because you saw yourself in the mirror?" he asked. "I'm so sorry I took you in there."

"No, it isn't that," I finally said. "It's because of what I heard, what I'm hearing."

"What? What do you hear?"

"Listen," and I began to sing along with the voice, which was slow and gentle.

He had never heard the song before, but when I got to the part: "Lead me, guide me, walk beside me, Help me find the way," he began crying too. I couldn't sing it again, but the song started over inside me anyway, filling me again with its warmth and love. I wept, and he wept, and we just looked at each other and felt love healing our wounds. For a few minutes that evening in my room, we shared something dearer than words could express. We cried as the voice of God sang to me. And somehow we both heard it.

This place of suffering and death became, for those moments, a place of holiness and reverence. Two rooms away a little girl had died the night before. In my room a voice from her world was speaking, and it spoke of love and peace. And *life*. I began to see clearly. My eyes opened all the way, and I began to see myself, truly, for the first time. Inside this mangled, tortured frame, I was a child of God. He would walk beside me, and I would find the way.

THE LOVE I FELT, KNOWING THAT THE LORD WAS NEAR, sustained me through the remainder of my stay in the hospital. Two weeks passed and I continued to get better despite more surgeries on my hands and face. Tendons were taken from my legs and sewn into my hands. Flesh was taken from my hips to create a new nose. My back soon looked like a plowed field from all the skin that had been removed. Like Humpty Dumpty, I was being put back together again.

My feet were healing and it was becoming easier for me to get around. I had made several more forays to the gift shop and had come back with more treasure for Whitey that we had secretly feasted on. But this ended abruptly when Whitey's candy wrappers were discovered under his mattress. The nurse who found them summoned me immediately to Whitey's room.

"RaNelle," she said. "What do you know about this?" She held out a fistful of wrappers.

"About what?" I said, glancing at Whitey who was lying there innocently counting the holes in the ceiling.

"Don't play with me, RaNelle. Have you been sneaking candy into the burn unit?"

"I may have brought *some* candy in," I said, guiltily, wondering how nurses punished their patients. Would they send me to bed without supper? Hog-tie me to the bed post?

"And you gave it to Whitey?" Her eyes could have melted stone.

"I thought it would help him—gain weight."

"RaNelle, you could have hurt his digestive system. He just had intestinal surgery. You know that!"

"But, he likes chocolate."

"That's irrelevant. We control his meals very carefully. What you did was wrong, RaNelle."

"I'm sorry," I said, though I wasn't sorry at all.

"And where did you get the candy, anyway?"

Here it comes, I thought. Time to confess. "I snuck out." It was barely a whisper.

"You *snuck out!* How in the world did you sneak out?"

"I went at night, when the nurse was asleep."

Her lips drew tightly over her teeth. "The nurse was *asleep?* Which nurse? Who was it?"

I was forced to tell the truth.

"You."

I saw a slight movement on the bed. Whitey's lips had pulled into a tight, almost painful smile. The rest of the room was monumentally still.

The nurse spoke again. "RaNelle, I'm disappointed in you. You really could have hurt him."

"I'm sorry."

I was dismissed and sent to my room. I didn't know if I was grounded or not.

After word got around, I became known as the escape artist of the burn unit.

Several days later I found out I would be going home. There was one skin graft left to do on my face, but it looked like I might be home for Thanksgiving. I would later return for surgery to restore my lips and would be travelling from California to Utah every other week for therapy, but at least I would be with my family.

Going home. I hardly knew what to think. More than anything I wanted to see my children again, but I was afraid of their reaction. I'd been gone six weeks. Would they accept me with my scars and new face? My mother had told me that when Terry returned it had taken a couple of days for Jason to feel comfortable around him. He was so young that I didn't know if he would even remember me.

And then there was Terry. I was still angry over the way he had left me on the mountain, seeming to care only for himself, and I was angry that he hadn't been with me more in the hospital. But I wasn't angry in the same way I had been before the accident. I was in a peculiar situation now. I was dependent on him. My injuries would take a long time to heal. I needed Terry. Maybe not to love me in the way I thought I should be loved, but to care for me, for my physical needs, and to help care for the children. What I thought I deserved didn't count for much now, so I was willing to accept something less than a perfect marriage. But the question kept surfacing, would he even be there for me?

There was one thing, however, I looked forward to with all my heart. In Bakersfield, we had our milk delivered, the old fashioned way, and I had grown accustomed to setting empty bottles out and finding them replaced by full ones in the morning. It was something I could count on. Life would be normal again, I figured, when I saw milk bottles on my porch once more.

Preparations for leaving the hospital included fitting me with a special mask that applied constant pressure to my skin grafts. Without pressure the scars shrink and wrinkle. It was called a Jobst mask—pronounced like the biblical character—and would keep my transplanted skin smooth while it healed, which could take years. I already had Jobst gloves for my hands, but the first time I saw the mask, my heart sank. It looked like an ugly, brown ski mask. It had been molded to fit the contours of my face and had velcro straps that connected behind the head. The nurses taught me how to apply Silvadine antiseptic ointment on my face and how to cover that with mesh bandages. The mask was the third layer. Changing the bandages under the mask and gloves was to become a daily routine.

The first time I put the mask on I asked if I could go to the mirror and have a look. The nurses smiled, recalling my last trip to the mirror, and one of them said, "Well, just this once."

I went to the bathroom and flipped on the light. I examined myself in the mirror, assessing side and front views and checking the holes for my eyes, nose, and mouth. I looked like a lipless bank robber. Then I said to myself, "Well, . . . you ain't pretty, but you're a heck of lot better looking than the last time I saw you."

Terry and my mother showed up to take me home. We would be flying by commercial airliner to California, where we would spend Thanksgiving at my parents' home. Jason and Christina were waiting for us there. Getting in another plane was the last thing I wanted to do, but because I couldn't endure a twelve-hour drive home, I either had to fly or wait another month.

Terry quietly busied himself with taking my things to the car while Mom helped me dress. She had brought me a sweat suit which covered most of my bandages and wraps, a welcome change from hospital gowns. I only had thick socks on my feet, so we planned to stop at a mall on the way to the airport to buy me some shoes. When I was ready, I made the rounds, saying good-bye to everyone—the patients who had been my companions through recovery, and the staff who had been my support. These doctors, nurses, and therapists had rescued me from death and had nurtured me back to life with skill and compassion. I considered them my friends.

Before going, I made a point of spending an extra minute with Whitey. He had been in the burn unit now for eight months, and I actually wished it were him leaving instead of me.

"I'm coming back for therapy you know," I told him. "And when I do, you and I are going to race around the whole burn unit, and you won't get any treats unless you beat me, do you hear?"

"Ha," he laughed in his faint, hoarse voice.

"Whitey, I love you." I bent down to kiss him. "You're the best friend I ever had." Tears lay on his cheeks. They were mine. "God bless you, Whitey," I said. "God bless you, forever." As I stood back up, I saw tears running from his own eyes and down into his ears. "You take care of them here, okay?" I said. He blinked, and more tears escaped. His arm moved, beckoning me closer. I got down by his face and heard a faint, hoarse voice. If it had been a little higher, it would have been mine six weeks ago.

"RaNelle, thank you," his wonderful, raspy voice said. "I love you."

I hugged him, crying on his shoulder. "Whitey, I'll miss you for the rest of my life." We held each other, and when I stood up, I noticed my mask was wet. "Oh no," I said. "I just got it, and I've already ruined it."

He laughed.

"Good-bye, Whitey."

"Good . . . bye . . . RaNelle."

I left the room and went back to Terry and Mom and the nurses. Nobody asked about the wet mask.

The staff walked us to the door of the burn unit, then everybody hugged me, gently, and we said good-bye. I was crying again, as were the staff members. I'll never forget their faces, bidding me farewell as Terry turned me to the door and out into the hallway. That final image of friends, not nurses or doctors, saying good-bye will stay with me forever.

We went down the elevator to the main floor, and instead of turning toward the gift shop as I had done several times late at night, we turned toward the large glass doors with EXIT over them. The rest of my life lay beyond those doors. Going through them was like emerging from a long dark night into day. But the day wasn't a bright one; the sky was slate gray, and sudden memories struck me of flying through clouds without vision. I lowered my eyes and saw snow on the ground. The hills were winter white. The slope was facing west, just as our mountain had been. Puddles of slush and mud completed the illusion, and I could have sworn I was looking at the crash site. I felt something like a flashback coming on, the terror of the mountain coming back. I closed my eyes and opened them again, and the feeling subsided. Mother was on one side of me, Terry on the other. We were approaching the parking lot.

"It's cold out, RaNelle," my mother said. "You may want this." She opened a large bag and pulled out a huge, blue parka. I stared as she held it up. It was gigantic. The hood was tentlike. The parka itself could have covered an NFL line-backer—with a place kicker or two thrown in. It was perfect. I pulled it on. Bandages, wraps, sweat suit, everything fit inside, and the best part was the hood that pulled almost all the way around my face. I wouldn't have to worry about my mask in public.

"Let's go," I said. "Where's the car?"

I didn't look at the mountains again on the way to the city. In fact, I didn't look at much of anything. The hood blocked my view. In minutes we were parking across the street from Crossroads Mall in downtown Salt Lake City. I got out and felt the cold through my stockings. "Ooo, let's get to the store," I said. "I can use those shoes right now." I closed the door and stepped around the clumps of snow littering the curb. My hood was tied down strategically, and a scarf circled around my neck and chin. Terry and Mom walked on either side of me as we headed toward the crosswalk.

Wind. People. Activity. Life. I was in The World again. My legs pumped up and down, like everybody else's. I was alive, back in the fabric of life, seeing cracks in the sidewalk, feeling the bracing wind on my nose and eyes. People walked past, went in doors, got in cars, ran across the street. I breathed hard, trying to keep up. We got to the crosswalk and waited for the light. Then something happened that defined, at least partially, the rest of my life.

A group of odd-looking teenagers stood on the opposite corner, waiting to cross. They were dressed in black leather, and the girls sported white makeup with black lipstick and heavy eyeliner. One girl had purple spiked hair and wore a dog collar around her neck. But the strangest one was a young man, perhaps six feet tall. His hair was bleached and stood in foot-long spikes down the middle of his head. The spikes were rigid, each one tapered to a chiseled point. They looked like defensive plates on a dinosaur. Twin tattoos graced the shaved sides of his head, and oversized safety pins hung from his ears. A green rubber snake coiled around his neck and ran up the side of his face.

The light turned green, but I was staring at the young man, mesmerized, and everyone started across but me. The young man stared at me in return as he came forward, and I realized my hood had fallen back. Terry pulled me into the street, and the two of us, the dinosaur and the burn victim, approached each other.

"Trying out for Friday the 13th?" he asked when we met in the middle. "Come on, Freddy, try an' take me!" he taunted.

"Let's go, RaNelle," Terry said, walking around the guy. Then I started giggling. By the time we got to the other side I was laughing hysterically.

"What's the matter with you?" Terry asked.

"Look at him!" I laughed, pointing. "He looks ridiculous!" I could hardly breathe I was laughing so hard.

From across the street the young man was still watching me, and I could see he was getting angry. "What's your problem?" he screamed. "Your face messed up? You deformed or somethin'?"

I caught my breath. "Yeah," I yelled back. "But it wasn't by choice! What's your excuse?" And I broke up again, laughing even harder, drool dripping on my mask.

Terry helped me into the mall and my mother quickly followed. We found a bench and sat for a moment while I calmed down. I tried to explain my behavior, but I couldn't make Terry understand. What had just happened in the street was important. It made me realize that I had not chosen my appearance as the kid had chosen his, and I had suddenly felt free of shame. If he could appear in public looking ridiculous by choice, then I could do the same by default. My mask had almost become a symbol of my innocence. Maybe I could even learn to wear it with pride.

We found the nearest shoe store, and after trying on several styles, I decided on a pair of high-top basketball shoes. They were large and a little clumsy, but I needed the high-tops for support. And after the experience in the street, I didn't care what anybody thought about me.

We left the mall and made our way back to the car. This time I didn't duck my head and stare at the sidewalk—I held my face high and enjoyed the view.

At the airport I received stares from every direction. Apparently my appearance created quite a stir with the authorities; four dark-suited security men soon intercepted me, asking which flight I was taking and demanding to know why I was wearing a ski mask. I said I was burned in a fire and would they like to see me with it off? They said no, apologized, and explained that they were just taking precautions. We were allowed to find our gate.

Everybody knows that the front of the plane is the most dangerous place in a crash. More people die there than in any other part of the plane. I asked for a seat in the front. "If we crash," I told Terry, "I don't want to survive. Surviving the last crash has about killed me." He chuckled. We got our seats and held on as the plane taxied down the runway gathering speed. My fingers were probably white under the wraps. With a sudden thrust the plane left the ground, and we were pushed back into our seats. Moments later I ventured a glance out the window and saw the brine-ridden waters of the Great Salt Lake racing beneath us. The plane banked, and the window I looked out of hung directly above the water. I held on, holding my breath, then the centrifugal force lessened as we leveled out, heading toward the sun over the

Nevada desert. I breathed again and tried to let myself believe that we would actually stay in the air all the way to Los Angeles.

The flight was uneventful, and my father picked us up and welcomed me back to sunny California. It was good to be back. Although this was the end of November, the weather was perfect, and everybody was in shirt sleeves. I even took my parka off and let the warm air flow against the tiny areas of my skin that weren't covered. As we drove I waited for somebody to bring up the subject of the damage my children had inflicted on my parents' home. Gratefully, it never came up. In fact, it would be years before my father even found out about the paintings. Yes, the Lord works in mysterious ways.

We drove up to the house, and I got out and went to the door. I was about to open it when my mother put her hand on my arm.

"RaNelle, I think you'd better stay here while I go in. Maybe it would be better if I talked to the children first and told them what to expect." The experience in the airport with the four men in suits had convinced her that the mask would be a bigger problem than she had thought. I waited outside on the porch while everyone else went in. It was the longest thirty seconds of my life. Then the door flew open and Christina was staring at me.

"Mommy?" she said, wide-eyed.

She was bigger than I had remembered and her hair was longer. I bent down to hug her. "Oh, Christina!" I said. "I missed you so much!" She jumped into my arms, and we embraced, and the tears began flowing.

I heard a small voice and looked up to see this little boy, almost twice as big as I remembered, staring at me from a few feet away. He had turned two while I was in the hospital.

His little voice squeaked out, "Mommy."

But when he saw my face he withdrew from me, his eyes widening.

"It's Mommy, Jason," I said. But he wouldn't come to me. He stood transfixed, and his body began to shake. "It's Mommy," I repeated, but he continued to shake. When Terry tried to explain who I was, he began screaming almost uncontrollably. I reached toward him, but, he turned from me and clung to my mother, burying his face in her pant leg. I was devastated.

My mother took Jason into the living room, and I greeted my brother and sisters who had waited at the house for me. Later, we sat and talked. Everyone filled me in on events in their lives since we had last been together. I listened, feeling exhaustion from the trip as well as sorrow over Jason's behavior. I was a new person to my family, an unknown, especially with the mask on. All I could do was let them see me, hear my voice, and decide if they still wanted me. Terry hovered around the room, listening to the conversation but never able to sit next to me. We talked about my stay in the hospital, the prospect of Terry finding work again, the rehabilitation that both of us would go through. Everybody was polite, but I could see the questions behind their eyes. Christina finally spoke the unspeakable.

"Are you my mommy—really?" she asked.

"Yes, honey. Remember how Grandma said I would be wearing a mask?"

"Yes," she nodded.

"I have to wear it to help my face get better."

"Take it off. I can't see you."

"You want me to take my mask off?"

Again she nodded, this time wordlessly.

I thought of the consequences. Seeing my scarred face, would Christina look at me in horror, as Jason had, and turn away? Then I decided that seeing me would have to happen sometime anyway. So I sat on the floor next to her and took the mask and bandages off.

Christina reached a finger toward me and gently touched my cheek.

"Owie?" she asked.

"Yes, I have owies. But they'll get better."

"Will they go away?"

"No, Christina, the scars will stay, but the hurt will go away."

I still had open sores on my face, but she knew better than to touch them. She felt all over my fuzzy head where hair was trying to grow back. It tickled her hand, and she laughed.

"Christina, would you like to help Mommy?" I asked.

"Yes."

"You can help me get my mask on every morning, okay?"

"You mean I can help you put it on?"

"Yes, if you're very careful. Can you be careful and help Mommy?"

"Yes."

"Okay, let's try it now."

She connected the Velcro straps in back just right. Then she put her finger inside the ear hole and pulled my ear out. Then she carefully, gently, did the other one. She rubbed my ears and made them feel better. When she was done she came around to the front and stared at me. She looked at my eyes and my nose and my mouth and my ears, and said, "Okay, let's do it again."

So we did. Four times. And right then Christina became the best helper I would ever have with my mask. Her hands were soft and delicate, yet strong enough to do each task. When we were through, we were more than mother and daughter; we were helper and patient. We were friends.

For as long as I was forced to wear the mask, I would see myself reflected over and over again in the eyes of curious and stunned observers. But it was the reflection of myself without the mask—in the eyes of my three-year-old daughter—that would remain in my heart. It made all the rest of it bearable.

Thanksgiving arrived and there was much to be grateful for. It was a celebration of sorts; everyone was relieved that we were together still. But all through the holiday Jason kept his distance. It was Christina who gave me an outlet for my love. She was constantly near me, telling me things that had happened at Grandma's house, asking me questions, stroking my gloved hand.

A few days later Terry and I piled the kids and luggage into the car and left for Bakersfield. We drove through the Tehachapi Mountains, traveling under the same skies where I had written my last will and testament. The world looked different down here, strikingly beautiful, peaceful. It is good to keep your feet on the ground, I thought. We wound down the Grapevine, the winding highway leading to the San Joaquin Valley, and saw Bakersfield in the distance. Home? As we drove through the streets leading to our neighborhood, everything looked changed, smaller, older. Then we drove up to our house, and I saw the milk bottles on the porch. Those glorious milk bottles! I reached down and touched one, feeling the rounded glass lip under my gloved finger. Memories. Security. Solid earth. They were just bottles, but they connected me to the dearest feelings of home and belonging.

We unloaded the car and got settled in the house. It was wonderful being home again. That night, exhausted, Terry and I put the children down, went to our room, and quietly changed our wraps before bed. We had hardly spoken since he picked me up at the hospital. At my parents' house we had occasionally caught ourselves looking at each other, unspoken thoughts traveling across the room. Who are you? Do you still love me? How do you feel about me? *How do I feel about you?* The rules of our relationship had changed. Divorce had come up, been decided upon, and now lay like a cleaver between us, unspoken of, untouched, unremoved. Love, if it ever lived again, would have to find a way to dull the biting edge of that decision. If love were not to live again, we would have a marriage of *de facto* divorce. He fell asleep, and I fell asleep, miles apart.

The next day, we started the difficult task of trying to make it on our own again. We made our own meals, changed diapers, bathed, answered the phone, changed our bandages, and soon I realized that I had romanticized the meaning of coming home. Living on your own is hard work when you have virtually no hands, no money, and no help. But my fears that Terry would not be there for me had been unfounded. He proved to be a great help, assisting with the housework and doing the shopping. And he was indispensable with the children, especially Jason who still avoided me. Out of necessity, Terry and I were evolving into a partnership.

I noticed my view of the world was changing. The more time went by, the more it seemed that everything around me was unreal. I had visited the beautiful world beyond this one and remembered it in vivid detail. These memories came into stark contrast now with my surroundings, and I began to feel the artificiality and lifelessness of everything I saw.

I went into the bathroom one morning and looked in the mirror. My face was a mirage, a chimera, my body an illusion. The mirror itself wasn't real. Each day, each night, I remembered my excursion to that world of light and love and color in the realm of the spirit. That world had been the most intensely real thing I had ever known. Sounds had vibrated in every part of my being. Colors had infused my body with happiness. Constant, surging love had filled me like warm, flowing water. In that world I had been alive, a part of everything, and everything was tangible and everlasting. But here, in this world, things were intangible, dead. The bathroom sink and counter were figments of the world's imagination. I took my Jobst glove off and touched them, trying to convince myself that they were actually there, and that I was there with them. Looking in the mirror I touched my face, the skin and scars, but I couldn't find me. Where was my spirit? The real me? I touched the faucet. It was more dead than my face. The metal seemed insubstantial and porous—just a notion of somebody's thought. My spirit could have seen through it. I reached out and touched the beige wall to my side. It was there, absolutely real, yet I knew it was a sham. My spirit, which was real, could walk right through it without effort. I yearned to pass through it now and emerge in that tangible, brilliant place which lay beyond these shadows. But my finger was blocked. It rested on the dead surface of the wall just above the towel rack. I was stuck, a prisoner in this lifeless vacuum.

I got dressed and went into the kitchen. Another counter hovered above the drawers. I reached out, and my finger stopped as I touched it. Yes, it was there, for now. I felt the door of the refrigerator. Another illusion. I went to the sink—another hovering lie, floating above the solid-looking cabinets and doors.

Then I looked out the window, and the sight literally took my breath away.

I saw spirit and light hiding in the camouflage of trees and sky, clouds, bushes, and grass. I saw light everywhere, spirit everywhere, straining to burst from behind its cloak of element. I ran to the front door, pulled it open and ran outside. A breeze hit my face. Life! Rose blossoms graced a gnarled, thorny bush. More life! The sky lay above me with hidden energy, and I could almost hear it whispering to me. I looked down and saw a mound of brown dirt where ants came and went, and I wanted to hold it in my hands and make sure it was there. I trembled with excitement as I got on my knees and peered at the meticulous hole with fine grains of sand built up around it.

Reality.

I went down the street, taking in the lawns and shrubs and dirt, and I wanted to embrace it all. This is real, I thought. This is spirit and light. This will endure.

I went back to the house, and inside I saw lithographs of paintings that hung on the walls. The paintings were masterworks of art, but the canvases they were on were dead. But only the canvases. The works themselves were as eternal as the spirit that created them. Each painting would live forever in the minds and hands of its creator. And thus I knew that all things we create here, for good or evil, will continue on within us, a part of our souls. But, I also knew that I had not purchased these paintings for the value of their creations or the power of their art; I had purchased them for the gratification of simply owning them, for the self-conceit of displaying them before friends and receiving their admiration.

I ate breakfast with the family and went back to the yard. I held a decaying leaf in my hand and saw virtue in it. The leaf's body would soon decompose. But life within it would continue to exist on the other side. Life could not be damaged or shortened or stopped. Life existed independent of its earthly disguise. It always was and always will be. I had existed independently of my body. I, too, always *was* and always *will be*, regardless of the abuse and ruin my body received. I would go on, perfectly, independently, eternally.

I paused for a moment and thought about my life before the accident and realized that I had almost lost the ability to touch virtue, to experience things that were real, such as faith and love and real happiness. Now I saw that life itself was virtue.

I went back in the house again and thought. I lay on the bed. I played with Christina. I watched Jason. And all the while I thought of my past—how I had lost touch with the most real part of myself, the goodness in me. I had lost affection for natural things. I had lost my childhood innocence, my pure love of pure things, and somewhere along the line I had even lost the dearest hope of my soul—my dreams. The paintings on the wall, as perfectly rendered as they were, told me that I had been faked out by the world, not because I had them, but because I had loved them as something greater than life, as possessions that somehow added to my self-worth. I realized that I had been deluded by false promises of honor, station, and money. The four walls spoke of my being deceived by a reality as porous as air. I realized that I had been suckered into cynicism. My creativity, my dreams had gone into the freezer of pessimism. My childhood had not died, it had been freeze-dried in the icy pursuit of praise and position. I had strangled the best part of my life with a cord meant to hoist me to the highest levels of acceptance, and I had been blind to my own execution.

I saw that Christina's love was pure, that Jason's fear of me was pure. My children were still untrammeled, willing to listen to themselves and respond without regard to outside expectations. *I am a child of God*, the song had said to me. Was I really willing to become a child again? Was I willing to let go of the things this world holds dear? Was I willing to embrace the innocence of life?

I wanted to go down to the beach and feel the sand between my toes. I wanted to feel the warmth of a star ninety million miles away reach up through the soles of my feet and satisfy the chill in my bones. I wanted to feel the sand, made up of rock billions of years old, form itself to the prints of my feet and stick to my skin and remind me that something on this planet is real. And I imagined that then I would gain a glimpse into that world where warmth and stars are eternal, where sand doesn't form to my feet because I step on it, but because it wants to. Because we are one and together.

Then a miracle happened, and I found that reality is what you make it. One day I was sitting in the living room by myself when Jason walked in and plopped himself on the floor in front of me. He had a handful of Hot Wheels, his favorite toy. I watched in silence as he took one of the cars and rolled it around the carpet, saying, "rum rum rum." He had loved playing with Hot Wheels since he had been old enough to hold one. He even slept with them at night. Then, without saying a word, he stood and brought the toy car over to me and put it in my lap. I was so surprised and pleased that I wanted to hug him, but I wasn't sure he'd let me. I saw that he was crying. He turned and ran back to the cars and sat down. Neither of us made a noise. Then he took another car and began playing with it, going "rum rum rum." Moments later he stood up and brought *it* to me and set it in my lap, still crying. He ran back to his cars and picked up another. He played with all the cars, bringing each one to me until they were all in my lap. Then he went to the middle of the room, sat down, and lowered his face. Tears dropped off his cheeks. I gathered the cars and took them to him, putting them all back in his lap, and I hugged him from behind. He took one of the cars and ran it on the floor again, saying "rum rum rum," and he let me hold him, and I kissed him on the cheek and said, "I love you, Jason." He started playing with the cars again, and in a few moments he had stopped crying.

And I had started.

The reality of life is found within the heart, within the home, within the arms of a Heavenly Father's embrace. But now, as I see things with a slightly clearer eye, I realize that reality can be found in everything if we view it right, even in walls and floors and countertops. Man-made things may not seem as real as God-made things, but there are times now when I see Jason with a car in his hand, and I think that Hot Wheels are the most real thing that ever existed. In fact, if they're not in heaven when I get there, I'll want to know why. Then I'll probably make a million of them for a son who proved to me that love *does* last forever, if you just wait long enough.

Chapter

FOURTEEN

E LIVED ON WELFARE THE NEXT FEW MONTHS. SINCE
Terry's hands were still healing, he had to wear Jobst
gloves which prevented him from working. He could hardly
hold a pencil, which didn't bode well for a mechanical
designer who worked mostly at a drafting table. He even had
difficulty holding the steering wheel in the car, but he went
out anyway, every day, looking for work. I grew to admire
him as he fought the pain every morning going out, knock-
ing on doors, and interviewing with prospective employers.
He may have been temporarily handicapped, but he wasn't
helpless. The last thing he was going to do was give up. Terry
was a fighter, which was exactly what we needed.

But we still hadn't talked about the accident or the decision to divorce. We lived in the same house and shared the
same last name, but we both knew that until these painful
gulfs were bridged we weren't really going to be husband and
wife. I knew Terry wanted to avoid these subjects. Whenever
the accident or my condition came up he would grow cold
and distant. At times I would see something unresolved brew-
ing in his eyes. If he would just talk to me, I often thought.
However, I knew that because of my own unresolved feelings,
I was not the one to offer help. Before the accident, I would
have confronted him. Now, for the sake of peace, I left it

alone. But I was convinced that the past would catch up to us if we didn't reconcile our feelings soon. Life could not simply go on as it had before.

Except for our trips to Salt Lake for therapy, I was confined to the house. We had no money and no insurance, but Terry and I still managed the fourteen-hour drive every two weeks to have the Jobst gloves refitted and to be trained in new exercises.

Christmas was nearing and people started bringing presents to the house. They'd ring the doorbell and leave food and toys and clothes on the porch. Everyone in the neighborhood must have left something. But what these good-hearted people didn't know was that I had bought our Christmas presents in September, prior to the accident. I had felt an impression to prepare for Christmas early, and everything was already bought and wrapped. But the presents kept coming, and soon we were deluged. So we tried to relax and let it happen. Christmas morning was a wonderful marathon. Seeing not only the gifts that friends had brought us, but also their goodness in remembering us, made us feel blessed beyond words.

Terry had exhausted every job possibility in Bakersfield and was looking now in Los Angeles, two hours away. He steered the car with a finger, or with his knees, because his hands still hurt so much. At night when we changed our bandages before bed, we compared the scars on our hands, and one night made a startling discovery. Our scars were beginning to resemble one another. Our hands were actually healing to look like matching pairs. "Look," Terry said one evening. "We have permanent matching mittens. I told you we were meant to be together." Although I resisted the easiness and convenience of this thought, I had to admit that there might be something to it. His words on the mountain had not been contrived and the scars on our hands were growing reminders of the miracles we had experienced. By all rights his entire body should have been consumed in the intense heat. It should have melted with the metal around him and flowed over the rocks and into the muddy earth beneath the fire. But only his hands were burned. Why was he spared so much pain and I wasn't? And how could he say we were to be together and yet remain so distant from me? I felt like I hardly knew him. If this were a marriage made in heaven, where was the heaven in our marriage?

Every day he looked for work and fought the pain. And every day I cared for the kids and fought the pain. Together, we just mostly fought the pain, silence becoming our most intimate conversation.

I began driving again, and I experienced the difficulty Terry had known. Holding the wheel was like holding a red-hot iron. I was a safe driver, but I had to force myself to grab the wheel tightly when turning and keep it steady while going down the street.

With both of us able to drive, we now needed our other car. We drove to the airport one day to pick up the car we had left before the flight to Utah. I wasn't prepared for what I would feel when Terry opened the hangar door. I saw the place where the plane once sat and I broke into sobs. It was here that I had felt the first impression not to buy the plane. Why hadn't I listened? That warm, little voice that told me to get presents early for Christmas was the same voice that had told me to not buy the plane, not to go on the trip, not to fly out of Salt Lake City in the storm, and finally not to fly out of Delta. But it was just fifteen minutes, we had reasoned. But it was just this or just that. It was just a little plane; we'll be careful. We'll take lessons and take precautions. It was just a little ways through the storm. We can beat the storm. We can beat the odds. But all we beat was our consciences. And now, standing in the empty hangar where that death machine once sat, I thought about what should have been, and I wept.

Oh, God, I thought, if I could just undo one of those decisions I would give all that I have, all that I am. One decision, and my face would be normal. One decision, and my body would function right. One decision, and we wouldn't be almost a million dollars in debt. Terry would be healthy. Our kids would have a normal mom and dad—if we worked things out. Oh, Lord, speak to me now and this time I'll listen . . . But the voice was silent. I had ignored it one too many times. And I broke down in sobs of remorse. Terry came to me and asked why I was crying, but I couldn't explain.

After a while he opened the trunk of the car in the hangar and began filling it. The tow bar for the plane went in, wheel blocks, cleaning bottles, towels, brushes, repair tools, the old door latch that wouldn't work. I watched and cried all the more. When it was all in the trunk, I got in the car and drove it home, taking all the reminders with me. I felt as though I could write a book called *If Only*.

A winter fog settled over the valley, keeping the sun hidden for weeks. Fog is as natural in the San Joaquin Valley as it is in London, and perhaps even more dense and suffocating. It condenses on everything, dripping from trees, walls, cars, and even from people who stay out in it too long. Sometimes the fog is so thick it muffles sounds, even the roar of trains and trucks. But even worse, it can muffle people's hopes and spirits for weeks at a time. The fog that invaded Bakersfield that winter was like that. It seemed symbolic of the greater fog that crept into our crippled lives. Terry and I couldn't see our future, and we couldn't feel the hope that should have illuminated at least a portion of our thoughts. Bills came in; of course we couldn't begin to pay them. Our church helped out with food and rent; and although the assistance was offered graciously, we couldn't help but feel less of ourselves for taking it. Although my spirit had seen the power and love of eternity, and although I still caught glimpses of it, the burdens and trials of this world continued to weigh me down. The fog of discouragement was beginning to condense on both of us like cold water. Even going out for a bite to eat was becoming difficult—and sometimes painful.

I took Christina and Jason to a fast-food restaurant one afternoon, where Christina and Jason enjoyed themselves on the playground outside while I waited in line to order. I had seen the manager staring at me from behind the counter, but he soon left and I didn't see him again. Suddenly my hands were pulled behind my back and handcuffs were snapped on. The manager turned me around and told me I was under citizen's arrest.

"What did I do?" I asked, shocked.

"Shut up and wait until the police come."

"But what did I do?"

"Just shut up and wait."

I began crying. "Please," I said, seeing the people backing away, "my children are here. Please let me go."

"Don't make another move, lady. Just wait here."

"But my kids, my kids!"

As we waited for the police I sobbed and prayed that my children wouldn't come in. The people hovered around, whispering, waiting to see what would happen. Several minutes later two policemen arrived.

"I've placed her under citizen's arrest," the manager said matter-of-factly.

"Why?" one of the policemen asked.

"She was going to hold us up. I was a security guard a few years ago, and I know why they wear these masks. She was waiting 'till she got to the counter."

"First," the policeman said, "get those handcuffs off her."

The manager hesitated.

"Now!"

The manager reluctantly put the key in and let my hands out.

"Ma'am," the policeman said, "are you okay?"

I rubbed my wrists. "I think so."

"Could you tell us why you're wearing the mask?"

I tried, not very successfully, to speak through the sobs. "I was burned, and I have to wear it, but he wouldn't let me explain." I undid the Velcro snaps and took the mask off. I felt like I was on stage. Some of the people gasped as the mask came off. "I was burned in a fire, and I have to wear the mask to help the skin grafts heal." My scars were raw, and my head was shaved.

"I'm sorry for the trouble, Ma'am," the policeman said. "You can put the mask back on." I began to put it on when I saw my children running toward me, concern on their faces. "It's okay," I said. "We have to leave now. We'll go eat somewhere else."

"What happened, Mommy?" Christina asked.

"Nothing, Honey. Come on, let's go."

Before we left, though, the manager stopped me and gave me two coupons. "I'm sorry for the inconvenience," he said sincerely, "but these will let you get your next two hamburgers free."

I didn't have an appropriate response, so I took the coupons and left the store. We didn't redeem them.

The fog was almost blinding now, just as it had been on the mountain. The emotional pain I endured was almost as great as the burning had been. And the pain wouldn't leave; it was ever-present, until early one morning that February.

We woke up early on the first Friday of the month, about 5:30, to prepare for another trip to Salt Lake for therapy. Terry was standing at the bedroom window.

"RaNelle," he said, "that house across the street is on fire."

It was still dark outside, and the fog was closing off the view to our fence, let alone to our neighbors' house which sat across a vacant field from us. But I hurried to the window. "See? Over there?" He pointed to where a yellow flame licked up out of the garage roof and illuminated the area around it. Shadows and light danced in three dimensions in the heavy fog. The moment I saw the flame I heard a voice in my mind. It was that voice I had asked to hear just one more time. It was clear and true.

"They're asleep. Get over there."

"Call 911!" I yelled to Terry as I threw on my sweats and ran for the door. "Tell them where to come." I ran out of the house and across the lawn barefoot, with no idea of what I was going to do. I got to the vacant lot and felt the gravel and rocks pounding into the soles of my feet and wished for my basketball shoes. The flames were rising higher now. An orange glow pierced the fog and glowed throughout the area. My foot must have hit something because suddenly I was falling face first. My hands shot forward and broke my fall, but I knew the instant I hit that I had broken open the newest skin grafts. I skidded and rolled through the gravel until I came to a stop, dazed. I got into a sitting position and again saw flames leaping from the roof. My mind whirled.

"Terry, get out! Get out!" I screamed.

I was on the mountain, and my hands were burning, and I couldn't get Terry out. "Please, Terry!" I screamed. "Get out!" I could see him leaning over the yoke of the plane as clearly as I could see the flames jumping above me. I beat the ground with my bloody hands, screaming at him, crying for him to get out. But he was motionless, and I was too far away to help, and the heat was scorching my hands.

Then the voice came to me again. *"RaNelle, get up and get them out of there. They're asleep."*

My confusion left. I saw that the flames were leaping off the roof, not the plane. As I got up, I noticed that one hand was bleeding where the new skin had torn. I ignored it and ran toward the house and saw the garage door opening. Were people trying to get out? Then the door closed again. Then it opened again. The heat was triggering the automatic door opener. Smoke poured out of the garage every time the door opened, and I knew I couldn't go in, so I ran to the front door and pounded on it. I rang the doorbell and pounded again, but no one responded. I tried to kick the door open, but it was too solid. I went over to the front window and considered breaking it, but I knew I couldn't walk over shards of glass with my bare feet; so I had no choice—I had to go through the garage. It was still opening and closing.

Inside, the garage was black with smoke, but I could make out two cars. Usually they had a third car out front, but it was gone. I guessed that the husband had already left for work. The cars were pinched into the garage so tightly, with other stuff against one of the walls, that I didn't know if I could get to the door leading into the house. I felt my way between the cars and heard the large door shut behind me. And I waited. It didn't open again. The automatic opener had failed. I was trapped. Smoke was already beginning to choke me, so I crouched low and tried to slip between the fenders of the two cars to get to the door, but they were too close together. I yelled and screamed at the house, but heard no response. I started coughing from the smoke and got lower. I had to do something fast, so I started banging on one of the cars. I may have been panicked, but it didn't occur to me that if they couldn't hear my screams, they certainly couldn't hear my banging on their car. I couldn't climb over the top of the cars to get to the door either, because that would take me up into the smoke. So I banged on the car—the small, old one, because I didn't want to dent the large, new car on the other side. It didn't occur to me that both cars would probably be going up in flames in a few minutes and it didn't matter which car I hit.

I kept banging and screaming, praying that someone would hear me. I wasn't just praying for the people in the house now, I was praying for myself; I was beginning to feel heat from the wall leading to the house. I was trapped unless somebody helped me.

A shrill, woman's voice screamed from the house.

"Your house is on fire!" I yelled.

The woman screamed again, closer to the door.

"Get out! Get out!" I yelled. I waited for the door to open, but nothing happened. The smoke was down to the floor now, and my eyes were burning and my throat was constricting. The fire in the plane welled up in my mind again, but I forced it down. I had to get out. No more screams came from the house, so I thought they had gone out another way. I went back to the large garage door and tried to push it open.

The door was warm and wouldn't budge. Flames had traveled to the roof. The air was jet black, and the heat was getting more intense. I lifted one leg to my chest and kicked as hard as I could, slamming my bare foot into the wooden door. Amazingly, the door popped open. I scrambled out under it and gasped for air on the driveway. The accident on the mountain was quickly falling behind me.

I went to the front yard expecting to find someone, but the door to the house was still closed, and the yard was empty. I felt like Samson now. I had just kicked open a huge locked door. I could do anything. I ran to the door, thinking I would kick it open as I had the garage door when suddenly it opened, and a woman came out. She looked at my face and screamed. I didn't have my mask on.

"What happened to you?" she cried. "Did the fire do that to you?"

"No, no! Did everyone get out?"

"No, my two girls are asleep in their room!"

"I'll get them," I said, trying to push past her. The smoke was billowing out of the house around us.

"You don't know where they are," she said. "I'll get them." She went in, and I followed her into the entryway.

"Stay low," I said. "Get under the smoke."

She went into the girls' room and came running out with the oldest one, about three years old. The girl was limp in her arms. She handed the girl to me and went back down the hallway. I took the girl out to the lawn, where I held her in my arms. She was breathing but couldn't seem to wake up. I rubbed her face and spoke to her. The woman ran out with a younger girl in her arms. Both girls opened their eyes and started coughing and crying. The woman and I looked at each other, stood up, and embraced, both of us crying.

"You saved our lives," she said. "Thank you, thank you."

"No," I said, looking at the flames over her shoulder and remembering another fire, "thank you."

"What? Why are you thanking me?" She looked at me with red eyes, partially from the smoke and partially from the emotions.

"It's a long story," I said.

We heard a siren and we went out to the street. I told her that Terry had called 911. The house was crackling in hot, angry flames and was already past saving.

An ambulance turned the corner and stopped in front of another house. We were surprised. Either that house was on fire too, or the driver was blind. As it turned out, the neighbor in that house had seen the flames and rushed down the stairs to help. He had slipped and fallen and broken his leg in three places. The ambulance was for him. A fire truck came around the corner seconds later.

Sometime in the commotion, we had introduced ourselves. Her name was Patty. Her husband, Bob, had indeed gone to work. He was about to get the most surprising phone call of his life. Terry ran up, and Patty thanked him for calling 911. All the firemen could do now was turn the water on and try to contain the blaze. The house was destroyed, but they were able to prevent the fire from spreading to adjoining houses.

News reporters came, asking questions, taking pictures, and within a few days I was in practically every paper and on every news show in the country. A local reporter, Diane Hardesty of the *Bakersfield Californian*, made the connection between the fire in the house and the fire on the mountain. She wrote a headline article that touched everybody, and the Associated Press and CNN carried it. The phone wouldn't stop ringing. Journalists and strangers called from around the world. Some of the media came to our house a couple of days later and told me to stay off the phone; somebody special was trying to get through. "Who?" I asked. They wouldn't tell me because they wanted it to be a surprise. But the phone kept ringing, one reporter after another asking me questions, and the person never did get through. President Reagan finally gave up and wrote me a letter.

The media found out about our financial plight and started a campaign to raise funds for our hospital bills. Appeals went out in newspaper, radio, and television ads. The same journalists who had written about the fire a few days before now wrote about our bills. That can be very humbling . . . or humiliating. But money began coming in, and we set up a special foundation for the funds. Terry and I sat back and said, "Wow."

The city threw a huge birthday party for me, officially christening my birthday *RaNelle Wallace Day.* Mayor Tom Payne awarded me the Mayor's Eagle Award for Heroism, citing me for bravery in saving the lives of three people. I tried to explain that all I did was get stuck in the garage and bang on their car, probably denting it severely. But it didn't matter, he said; the car ended up in ashes, along with the other one, and nobody knew about the dents. The media asked questions for hours, it seemed, and the story went out on the wire services again.

I was named California Woman of the Year, and tens of thousands of dollars came in, allowing us to pay many of our bills. A miracle had truly happened in our lives. And not just in *our* lives. Bob and Patty experienced something of a blessing in disguise—if you can call good fortune after your house burns down a blessing. The fire had started because of a faulty water heater, one which was guaranteed, and because they also had full renters' insurance they got a huge settlement and were able to buy a new home, new cars, and replace most of what they lost. Although they couldn't replace heirlooms and pictures and important papers, at least there was something of a silver lining in the tragedy. After they bought their house, Patty said to me: "RaNelle, it was a blessing for you *and* me. God meant it for us both."

Terry and I had been given enough money through the generosity of strangers to cover many of our medical bills. I had faced my worst fear—the fear of burning again—and had wrestled it into absolute subjection and in the process had blessed someone else. But perhaps the greatest blessing for me was the knowledge that God had blessed me with that still, small voice again, the voice that burned within me. And this time, I had listened to it.

F I F T E E N

A YEAR AND A HALF AFTER THE ACCIDENT THE DOCTOR told me I needed to have a hysterectomy. He found a polyp on my cervix, cysts on both ovaries, (one the size of a grapefruit), tumors on my uterus, and now endometriosis was covering the outer uterine wall. My suffering over the past year and a half had gradually shifted from my skin and tissues to my internal organs, creating a very different but almost unbearable pain in my abdomen before each menstrual cycle. I found myself lying on the bed trying to breathe through the cramping as my abdomen would swell with blood for a week. Before the blood was released, my abdomen would swell to make me appear six months pregnant.

All the fears of Doctor Saffel in Salt Lake were coming true. The stress of the burns had caused my body to begin shutting down internally—in some cases even withdrawing its natural defense systems, in other cases actually attacking organs. Since the endometriosis had begun to spread to the ovaries, my general practitioner felt I should have a hysterectomy soon. I thought back to Whitey and how the stress from his burns had caused his bowels to burst, nearly killing him. The endometriosis hadn't settled on my bowels yet as far as we knew, but it was probably just a matter of time before it caused such damage to other organs that a full hysterectomy would become mandatory rather than optional. I told the doctor I wanted two other opinions.

The first expert I needed to consult was myself. Did I really want another child? The answer was an unequivocal yes; even if I hadn't had the near death experience I would still have wanted more children. The experience just added an urgency to the desire. The second question was more difficult to answer. Did Terry and I want another child? We had established that we needed each other, but we weren't sure at all that we loved each other. If need disappeared, without love our relationship would have nothing. But Terry was willing to have another child, and time was running out; if we were going to do it, we had to do it soon. I just prayed that Terry and I could work out our problems and stay together.

After making that decision, I went to an OB-GYN in southern California. He echoed the first opinion and told me to have the operation immediately. "Forget having more children," he said. "You've already got two kids. That's enough. It's more than some people ever get. Just get on with your life." I thanked him and made an appointment with another OB-GYN, a fertility specialist. He was young, right out of his residency. "Please work with me," I said. "I want to have another baby more than anything in the world, and if there's any way we can relieve the pain and take care of these other problems without having a hysterectomy, I want to try it." He was dubious but was willing to try alternative approaches. First he gave me an array of drugs to arrest the growth of the tumors and endometriosis. We tried them for six months without success. The pain continued, and I wasn't successful in getting pregnant. Then he decided to operate to remove the ovarian cysts. The operation, he said, had less than a fifty-fifty chance of success, but he would try if I wanted him to. I couldn't see another option except a hysterectomy.

The operation took six hours, and the doctor ended up reconstructing one of the ovaries. He thought the operation had gone well but didn't know if the ovary would function again. Only time would tell. He put me on fertility and other drugs to fight the tumors and endometriosis. I hoped for the best but gradually fell into discouragement as weeks slipped into months without results. Then suddenly new hope came.

That summer a fireman named Adam Graehl organized a river rafting trip for burn victims, supported by a local fire department. I had been helping fire departments and school systems create fire prevention programs for children over the last several months. My publicity—and mask—made me easily recognizable to both adults and children, and my new passion for preventing burns happening to anybody else made me determined to crusade as hard and as long as my body would let me. On the rafting trip I met a *real* celebrity, somebody who would end up affecting my life deeply. Holly Holstrom, a model from *The Price is Right*, came along to help support the firemen and children. She had done service work with burn survivors in the Sherman Oaks hospital where I had undergone some therapy, but she and I hadn't met until then. We seemed naturally drawn toward each other, and before long I found myself opening up to her. After telling her a little about my near-death experience, I learned that she too had experienced one. But as we were talking, she finally said, "RaNelle, there's something you're not telling me about your experience." I looked at her, not knowing what she meant. "Most people don't want to come back. Why did you choose to come back?"

I paused, knowing that my reason might surprise her, but I decided to open up all the way. "I have a child waiting for me. I came back to give him birth."

She understood immediately. "So, are you going to have this child soon, or are you waiting?"

When I told her about the problems I was having, she gave me some advice: "What you need to do is to stop listening to those doctors and start listening to your own body. First, get rid of those drugs the doctor is giving you. You've already tried them long enough and they're not working." It seemed a radical thing to do, but she was right. The drugs weren't working.

Next, she told me to "clean out my system" and start eating right. She was a vegetarian and gave me the name of a health-food store in Sherman Oaks. She also gave me a list of things to get and concluded with these words of encouragement: "If you do this, RaNelle, I think you'll be pleased. I even bet you'll get pregnant right away. If there's a child waiting for you, he'll find a way to get here."

I was impressed. Holly seemed to know what she was talking about, so I went home and got rid of the medicine then bought the natural foods she had recommended. I got off the preservatives, all the junk foods, and went completely natural. About a month and a half later my body told me that something had changed.

I went in and saw the OB-GYN and told him I thought I was pregnant. He was doubtful. "Are you aware of the term 'hysterical pregnancy?'" he asked. It sounded like a psychosomatic illness to me, which may have been something *he* had, but it wasn't something *I* had. I knew I was pregnant. But he was leery. "I want a pregnancy test," I said.

"Let's wait," was his response. "If the symptoms continue, see me in a month or two."

I went home and got on the phone to the lab that his office used for tests. "Hello, this is so-and-so," I said, giving the name of one of my doctor's nurses. "I need to order a pregnancy test for a patient—RaNelle Wallace. May she come down this afternoon? The doctor would like to get the results ASAP."

"Sure. She can come in any time."

"Thank you very much. I'll inform her. Good-bye."

I was in the lab getting the test an hour later, no questions asked. The technician said he'd get the results to the doctor before the end of the day. I was so excited I almost went in to the doctor's office to get the results myself. About closing time I got a call. It was the doctor.

"Are you ready for some good news?" he asked.

"Sure."

"You're pregnant!"

"Imagine that."

"We just got the results back. I have to admit I thought it was all in your head. Well, congratulations, RaNelle. Glad I could help. We'll want to see you soon for a prenatal exam."

He never did bring up the test, and I never told him that it wasn't his drugs that were responsible for my getting pregnant. I called Holly right away.

"What did I tell you, RaNelle? Congratulations. I hope it's a boy."

"Of course it's a boy," I said. What else could it be? I had already seen him. I already knew his name.

Eight months later I went into labor and had a wonderful, healthy baby girl.

I was astonished. This wasn't the way it was supposed to be. Somebody had pulled a switch on me!

We named her Danielle, and she and I immediately had more than a mother-daughter bond; from the beginning, it was a bond of friends. I began to recognize the kind of bond I had shared within a circle of spirit friends. One of them had clung to me, vowing that she would never leave me. Could she be my darling daughter? There are times when she still clings to me, almost desperately, and although it can be exasperating when I want to do something else, I see the look in her eyes that reminds me of a former world. We have been friends for a long, long time.

Now I had some thinking to do. Did I want to go through all this again? The pregnancy had not been a pleasant experience with all my other problems exacerbating the distress of pregnancy and delivery. The doctor wasn't even sure I could have another child as I was developing another cyst on my left ovary. "If you think you can have another baby," he told me, "you better do it right away because the endometriosis and cysts won't stop growing."

But the endometriosis and cysts weren't my only concerns. Terry and I were having problems again. Suppressed emotions in the aftermath of the accident were coming to the surface in heated arguments. Occasionally Terry had professed love for me. But now I knew what love was. And this wasn't it. In spite of my efforts to maintain peace, we returned to our old methods of handling differences, and our life together was filled once again with bickering. And when I thought everything would fall apart, Terry announced that he, again, wanted to move to Utah. In our spare time, and before our new troubles began, we had designed a large, beautiful house, something that would fit perfectly in the modern yet rugged look of Park City. But I never thought that we would follow through with actually building it. Terry was doing extremely well in his work now. Though his hands were still healing, he was able to use them well enough, and he was quickly becoming one of the few mechanical engineers who understood the latest software technologies in drafting and was finding himself in demand by many industries. Getting a job in Utah would be no problem for him, but I was extremely uneasy about trying to make the move again—I had never felt peaceful about it, and now was no exception. But another thought occurred to me: what if this is all Terry needs to make his life complete? What if building the house and moving to the land of his dreams will finally help him discover his hidden dimensions? Perhaps sacrificing my own feelings just one more time would make a difference. Perhaps giving him this would make him love me more. So I told him I would do it, and like a whirlwind he quit his job and we were packing for Utah. My head spun from the speed of it. Once in Utah, we rented while Terry established himself in his new work, then we took out a loan we really couldn't afford and built our dream home.

But my heart sank as I realized that things had remained tragically the same. I had sacrificed my dreams to allow him to pursue his, and his dreams didn't seem to include including me more. I felt I had moved to Utah for the wrong reasons and realized with a sense of dread that I was locked, again, in this cycle of unreciprocated sacrifice. Or at least it seemed that way to me.

When I brought this up he expressed love and concern for me, but how could I accept his occasional statements of love in the face of near constant battles over everything from money to trust to faith in God? He was a wonderful father, and in many ways a great husband—dependable, faithful, hard-working, humorous, energetic—but despite his words on the mountain that we were meant for each other, I still couldn't seem to get along with him. It was that simple. And it wasn't a secret either. Old friends would see us and say, "Wow, are you two still together? I can hardly believe it. When are you guys getting a divorce?" Not exactly the kind of greeting you expected. But these friends were only expressing the view most people had about us.

I was as lost as I had ever been. Things had seemed so easy on the other side. Right decisions were obvious. Love and tolerance were everywhere, filling me, making most decisions easy. While I was there I couldn't believe the childishness of some of my actions here, the pettiness of some of my priorities, the words and deeds that had hurt myself and others. While I was there I couldn't believe that I would ever revert to such behavior again. Yet now I was doing it. I had learned a great deal—but not enough. A wise man once said, "To know and not to do is not yet to know." I guess deep down inside I still didn't know. And as I thought about it, I realized that this was exactly right. I simply didn't know what to do. If I knew, I would do it. Should Terry and I be together? Should we divorce? Should we try to have another child, hoping it would be a boy? What was right? On the other side choices were so clear they were obvious. Here, the world gets in the way, pushing you against your will—sometimes for the better, sometimes for the worse.

The world did that for me now, pushing me toward something I wasn't ready for. I found that I had become pregnant again. I was distressed and deeply discouraged. I hadn't planned for this, but now I had to face new facts. Life wasn't going to stop because I didn't know what to do. Sometimes lessons have to be learned and relearned and relearned. I felt that I was a stronger person for the things I had experienced, but I still didn't have all the answers. Knowing what is real in life doesn't mean knowing what to do about it. Knowing that there is a God in the universe doesn't mean having his wisdom. Knowing that love is the key doesn't mean always knowing how to turn it.

I hated that I was pregnant, and soon I felt that it was a mistake. I didn't believe this infant could be that choice person I had met on the other side; the circumstances surrounding this whole situation seemed wrong for that, but what should I do? I did not want to have Terry's child, but again, what could I do?

Mistake or not, I had to go ahead with it. The child would be born, and I would do the best I could to provide a home for it. I was angry, and I was depressed, but I would not abort this life within me. So I kept eating and worrying and arguing with myself. And as the arguments went in circles, round and round with no answers, I ballooned to all-time highs on the scales. I guess my children just figured that the weight came with the pregnancy because they never mentioned it, but most of my family and friends knew better. I was obviously a very unhappy person.

I looked like a short walrus by the time I went into labor. The baby was coming a couple of weeks early, and Terry was out in California, but he said he would get back right away. I wasn't ready at home yet, so my mother, who had come back to visit me, drove around that evening buying things and making arrangements for the care of the children. The contractions had become intermittent, stopping for hours at a time. The next morning Mom and I drove to the hospital in Salt Lake, but the contractions stopped again, and we ended up waiting in the hospital, talking with each other and with my coach, Annie. Terry showed up, dead tired from driving all night, and for lack of anything else to do, he came in and listened to us. Hours went by, and we ended up sharing many personal stories, some rather ugly and painful. Annie shared a couple of experiences about her friends and abuse in their childhood, and I noticed Terry listening closely. When she finished, she was in tears, and so was Terry. I was amazed. I had only seen him cry once before, and it hadn't been in compassion for somebody else. As the contractions finally started getting closer I asked him to stay behind as I went into the delivery room.

"It'll be Nathaniel," he said as they wheeled me out. I was actually sorry for Terry. He couldn't see that Nathaniel would not come into a situation like this; too much depended on his life's mission. Nathaniel would need the stability of a strong family.

My abdomen looked like a boxing match was going on inside as the baby twisted and turned. It would get into position then fight and twist away again. Annie tried to keep me relaxed and breathing right, but it was a losing effort; the labor pains left me exhausted, breathing in long, agonized moans. Eventually I forgot about breathing right; I just wanted that baby out. After a couple of hours, Annie and the nurses found some reason to leave me alone and stepped out of the room. It was about four o'clock on Sunday afternoon, August 22, 1992. The soundtrack from *Somewhere in Time* was playing on a stereo near my bed, the beautiful, haunting melody of a story of love beyond this life. As this music soothed me between contractions, an impression came that I was being watched from my right side. I turned and saw a man standing there, a tall man with dark hair and blue eyes. He was dressed in a white suit. Was I seeing things? I closed my eyes and looked again, and the young man was still there, next to me. His eyes were wide and mournful. I had seen those eyes before, those sorrowful eyes. But now he was lamenting the pain I was going through, the suffering I was experiencing for him. He opened his mouth and said, "Thank you, Mom," and a wave of love came into me that blew my spirit into a spin. I looked at him through tears and said, "Thank you." Then he was gone.

The baby finally settled down and the contractions became consistent. The nurses and Annie returned. Terry also came in and stood against a wall at the far end of the room. I gave a final push and heard a little cry. Annie said, "You've got a beautiful baby boy, RaNelle. I hope you've got a name for him."

Terry came forward and looked at the baby, and Annie let him clip the cord. "It's Nathaniel, isn't it?" he said.

I nodded, still crying.

Chapter

S I X T E E N

NATHANIEL'S BIRTH HAD BEGUN TO CHANGE TERRY, AND a month later he and I began counseling and started discovering reasons for the hurtful things we had done and words we had said. The accident was finally brought into the open, both with the counselor and in private, and we began to understand why the emotional wounds had lingered so long. One night Terry shared his experience on the mountain, and I began to realize that we had gone through two very different ordeals that day.

Just before we crashed, he said, he was frantically working the controls when he realized that he was about to die. "This is it," he thought, "I'm going to be smashed against the rocks." Then he saw a strong, translucent hand and wrist come out in front of him from above his shoulder. The hand then pressed against his chest, holding him against the seat. "A warm, tingling feeling came over me," he said, "and I knew I wasn't going to die." He saw the plane ignite before it stopped sliding, and he began tearing at his seat belt. "When you kicked open the door," he told me, "it felt like a flamethrower lighted on my face from the right side. I couldn't get my seat belt off, so I ducked my head and prayed. Then I lost consciousness." He had no recollection of the next five minutes. He didn't feel the heat as the plane burned down around him, and he didn't hear me screaming on the wing. "I don't remember anything," he said, "until a small voice said to me: 'Sitting is suicide. Get out.' I reached down and unlatched the seat belt, which had been impossible to unlatch minutes before. The wonderful feeling stayed. I looked through the flames encircling me and saw you standing on the wing as clearly as if you were next to me, and I knew you were burned and needed help. Then the next thing I knew I was in front of you on the wing. I don't remember getting out of the plane or walking through the fire. I just felt myself in a wonderful, peaceful daze. Then two thoughts were in my mind: The Lord had heard your prayer, and he wanted us to be together."

I sat in amazement as Terry told me this. God had literally spared his life. Although he didn't remember being helped out of the flames, he had raised his right arm as if being led by someone, then had distinctly said to me on the wing: "Where is the man that helped me out? Did you see him?" The plane had burned all around him, but he didn't receive any injuries at all, except to his hands, and his scars were almost identical to mine now—our twin gloves. Yes, he had received divine intervention in getting out of the plane, but moments later I realized that this wasn't what had concerned me, this wasn't what had bothered me over the years. If we were supposed to be together, why did he walk away, why did he leave me on the mountain?

"I didn't leave you up there," he countered. "When I came back to you, you always stopped. You were giving up. I couldn't carry you all the way, so I had to keep you walking, and I never did lose sight of you. Every time I checked, you were there, still following. And this warm, peaceful feeling stayed with me. I knew exactly where to go at every turn. At every fork and at every trail a comforting feeling came over me as I decided on the right direction, and I wanted to get there as fast as possible. I know I should have helped you more. I should have given you my coat or my shoes, but at the time all I could think of was getting down that mountain and following that feeling. RaNelle, I've got more than enough guilt to last me a lifetime; I should have never gotten us up there in the first place. You were right; we shouldn't have gone. We should have followed your feelings. We should have stayed home. And on the way down the mountain I suppose I was running away from all that, as much as I was running toward help. I was running away from what I had done to you. I'm sorry, RaNelle. I did the best I could in getting us down, but I'm sorry for what I've done to you."

God uses people's weaknesses sometimes to accomplish his purposes. He used Terry's weaknesses, as well as his strengths, to get us down that mountain. Terry was right, I would not have made it if he hadn't gone ahead and made me follow. It gave me a goal—to follow him, to not be left behind—and I pursued that goal until I dropped. The sheriff followed our tracks up the mountain the next day and found that we had walked five miles down the mountain in virtually a straight line to the road, although we had no idea in which direction the road lay. Terry had indeed been led.

"Do you remember when I took your hand in the theater, in Delta?" he asked.

"Yes."

"I didn't want to leave you. I wanted to put our marriage all back together."

That's true, I thought. He didn't want to leave me after all, but then a realization came to me. "No Terry, that's been the problem all along. One moment you want to walk away, and another moment you want to put it all back together. There's no stability in that. I can't count on you."

"I'm still here, aren't I? You can count on me to keep trying."

"But how long, Terry? How long before we stop trying and actually get there?"

"I don't know. All I can do is keep trying."

I thought about this a moment then remembered another voice from the past. "Keep walking, RaNelle. Keep going, keep trying. Just follow Terry's feet." And I followed him and suffered and fought until I got to the road. And then I learned that when you've reached the point of no return and think you can't endure any more, you can still keep going. You can always take one more step.

"All right, Terry," I said, resolving to follow him, to walk as far as he could. "I'll keep trying too. I'll try to make this marriage work if you will, but there's one thing I think we ought to do."

"What, go to another counselor?" he asked warily.

"No."

He eyed me another moment, and I saw concern. "Wait a minute, RaNelle, is this another one of your premonitions?"

"And what if it is?" I felt the makings of a fight.

He smiled. "Then I guess we better follow it, whatever it is."

I smiled too, stretching the tissue that had been grafted into my new lips. "You know what, Terry?" I asked, touching my finger to my mouth.

"What?"

"Sometimes it really hurts to smile."

He laughed and stood up. "Well, then, get ready for some serious pain." And he took me in his arms and gently kissed me.

There's been a tingle ever since.

Returning to the crash site was the one thing I thought Terry and I should do. That mountain had loomed over us like a vulture waiting for a carcass. It had shadowed every word, lingered in almost every thought, preying upon us by day, dancing with us by night. The mountain was our mutual alter ego, our united shadow that crippled our dreams and hopes for the future. As long as the mountain loomed over us we would never love or trust each other completely. I knew that we had to go back and climb it, going up the same way we had come down, find the crash site, and put it beneath our feet. Terry and I would stare it down together.

We had been told that townspeople had stood outside their homes the day after the accident and looked at the crash site through binoculars as a plume of smoke rose from the mountains. Terry and I now pulled over to the side of Interstate 15, about a mile south of Fillmore, and looked toward the mountain for the crash site, but we only saw snow-capped peaks. Christina and Jason, the children who had lived through their own tragedies resulting from the crash, were with us. Their challenges were still continuing. Only recently they had seen me removed from a clothing store in a mall because my appearance was upsetting customers. They had seen the horrified looks of their friends and teachers when I visited them at school. And, of course they had seen their mother get arrested and handcuffed because of the fear her face had caused.

The four of us stood by the fence now, the fence Terry and I had once fought to get over. Our car rested on the very ground the ambulance had been parked on. We climbed over the fence and walked across the dirt road to the next fence, the one that had taken us a lifetime to get through. We quickly got over it too. We had water and food with us, and we wore shoes and long pants. We were ready this time.

Going up was a lot easier than coming down had been. We found the old washed-out road and went by the outhouse and saw grass growing up through the toilet seat. I had thought we would be rescued here and had wanted to stop. I almost certainly would have died if Terry had let me rest for a few minutes. We saw the old beer can that had inspired me to yell, "Look for the drunk! Look for the drunk!" I had actually believed that a wasted, bearded man was hanging around somewhere and could help us if we just found him. The can looked no worse than it did that day years ago. Beer cans are tenacious. We got over the next barbed wire fence, and the next, the one I had left part of my hand on. The strands of wire gave us no trouble at all. Now up we went through the maze of jagged boulders where I had tried to run and had finally fallen, tearing open my leg and partially dislocating my hip. I could hardly believe that I had actually run on these rocks barefoot. The pain from the burns had driven me insane. The mountain got steeper, and we had to stop a few times to rest. The children were doing well, talking to us, asking questions, trying to see what we saw.

Two hours after leaving the car we came over a little rise of boulders and there it was. We gazed upward at a swath through the trees that resembled a firebreak. The children went ahead, picking their way through the jagged rocks. I lingered behind, unable to speak, with sudden sensations rising that had lain dormant for years. The mountain almost seemed to possess a voice.

As I arrived at the crash site, the children were bending over, sifting through pieces of metal. I walked up to the point where I had kicked the door open and the fire had blasted me. Charred scraps of aluminum from the plane littered the ground. I stood between the boulders that had been sticking

up through the bottom of the aircraft. To my left I saw
something shiny on the ground. A little pile of coins lay
under a small tuft of grass. The change had been in my
purse. We hadn't noticed that it was gone when we came
down the mountain. A sudden thought hit me. Terry had
also lost his wallet in the crash, losing what had been left of
the three thousand dollars, our total worth at the time. But
as I looked, I saw only globs of metal lying on the ground
like silver ingots, once boiling from the intense heat. The
coins had survived, but the wallet with the paper money had
been destroyed.

Firefighters had hauled most of the plane's carcass away
years ago, leaving only bits and scraps of reminders, but they
were enough to trigger repressed memories. The voice spoke
louder, and strange feelings rose in my chest, heavy, loud feelings that had no meaning and no source. I went off a short
ways and found a rock to sit on. I tried to control, or at least
understand, the pounding inside me. I saw my children and
Terry sifting through the wreckage, and something about it
seemed familiar. This is where I had been on fire. This is
where I had half fallen and half climbed off the wing. This
is the very rock where I had prayed to God for help and had
seen Terry come out of the flames. My whole body tingled,
and the voice grew and became a chorus of maddening,
screaming voices. I sat for minutes not thinking, just letting
the waves of sound and emotion roll through me. In the distance below lay the valley where Fillmore and Delta rested in
the sun, but I didn't see it. To my left and right rose snow-
capped peaks, but I didn't see them. I didn't see anything for
several minutes, until the internal voices and rushing emotions subsided, and then I opened my eyes—eyes that had
already been open.

I saw a graveyard. This is where I had died. This is where I had come face to face with eternity. I felt the spirit of what I had once been, lying in the ashes, hovering over the rocks. And I recognized one of the voices speaking inside me; it belonged to a potential TV news anchorwoman, her unblemished face smiling, a voice to reach the world. The image was dead now, yet her voice lingered, trailing in the air like smoke. I heard another voice, more elusive, a voice that still tried to cry out from time to time. It was the arrogance of a girl untouched by the hammer of life. It was the impertinence, the cockiness that gave her power to dismiss danger, to ignore warnings, to set her face in a direction that would shatter lives. The voice was only a whisper now, a raspy, lingering cry from the past. I had been hammered by the smith of consequence; I had been refined by the bellows of remorse. If pride lifted its head in me again, I would show it the scarred face of a previous victim and let reason win. Consequence could engender a rare and permanent humility.

I also heard voices of conflict with Terry. I sat on the rock and heard the old decision of divorce still ringing within me. The determination to endure alone had driven fresh purpose into me. But the wrenching of cause and effect had changed hearts. No, Terry and I would not divorce. Our commitment to our marriage was stronger, after all, than our differences. Deep inside, under the layers of pride and weakness, we had both found genuine commitment toward each other and the family. As Terry had become more sensitive to my needs, I had seen a hidden giant emerge—a man with a heart of gold, a faithful, determined soul, committed to keeping the family together. Now he was becoming more comfortable in showing this wonderful side more often, and as this giant began to emerge, I found myself falling in love with him all over again.

As I realized just how committed he was to me, I found my love growing deeper each day. Commitment was the key to our love, and love was the key to our future. His strange words after the fire were proving more prophetic each day. We *were* meant to be together. Like the last wisps of smoke, the distant voices of doubt were fading.

All these voices rose within me, and one by one I buried them. I buried my once-whole self. I would not have that face again, and I would not accept its continuing desire for praise or the ease which it could have afforded. Unlike the ancient queen, I would not fool myself with any kind of vanity, even the vanity of accomplishment. I would cherish my scarred face and gnarled fingers because they were the only face and fingers I had. I would not fight them or run from them again. I buried the whisperings of regret. I would not waste my time gnawing on the might-have-beens of my life. Yes, I could write a book called *If Only,* but I wouldn't. I would write a book each day on the hearts of my children. My works would be my pen. I buried my pride and years of self-deception spent thinking I could do anything. I buried my discouragement and years of self-pity thinking I could do nothing. I would not kid myself again. The consequences of self-deception and self-indulgence hurt too much.

I buried the dreams of my past and embraced a new idea. I would teach. People had always told me I could do two things extremely well: I could cook, and I could talk. As for the cooking, I had won the Betty Crocker national baking contest while in high school, but that wouldn't get me very far now. So I had to rely on my talking, which meant I had to learn how to speak correctly and effectively. I would train myself to reach the heart of anyone who would listen. I would share the marvelous love I had felt and the lessons I had learned. And I would make it my life's goal to personify the endurance and compassion I preached, allowing me to teach both by word and example.

So I buried my visions of fame and riches, my visions of *me*, and embraced a dream of sharing.

Already, I reflected, my heart had taken me in new directions, adding a quiet richness to my life. I had overcome my fear of "getting involved" and had worked with hospitals and schools and different churches in teaching burn prevention and fire safety. Several of the hospitals in southern California had allowed me to serve as a trauma counselor for burn survivors, and, as happens so often with service, I had gained far more than the people I had counseled. One couple I remembered well had been in a plane crash with uncannily similar circumstances to ours—the husband and wife even looked like Terry and me—only in this crash four people had been involved and the pilot's parents had been killed. While I spoke to the pilot, I saw Terry all over again. I saw his pain, felt his grief, and knew that he was blaming himself for everything that had happened. "It was just an accident," I said to him over and over, and every time I said it I felt myself freeing Terry from the blame of our accident. "But it's my fault. It's my fault," he repeated, and I hugged him, almost feeling Terry in my arms, and said, "No, it was just an accident. You've got to free yourself from the guilt. You did the best you could. You are not to blame." And I felt absolution, understanding, well up in me for Terry.

Then I went to the wife, who was burned on her face and hands just as I had been, and tried to comfort her. Although she was a nurse, nothing she had seen at work had prepared her for the pain of her burns or the fear of permanent disfigurement. She was disappointed in her husband. He had stayed with the plane and his dead parents while she walked miles, with no shoes, to find help. I told her to be patient and kind toward him. "He's suffering greater guilt over this than you know," I said. "You've got to love him, help him through this. You've got to forgive him as soon as you can, or your relationship will be crippled forever." And again I saw Terry and me and knew that I had just spoken to myself. Of course, I couldn't make the young woman forgive her husband, or her husband forgive himself, they would have to do that on their own, but I could feel the truth of my advice and apply it to my own life. Our counselor had given me this advice before, but I couldn't hear it. Now it rang as clear as a bell. I had to completely forgive Terry, and he had to forgive himself before we could be whole as husband and wife.

I went home that night and hugged Terry and told him I loved him, and I felt the tingle again. I told him I was sorry for the blame I had held over him. I saw shock on his face, then, finally, relief and acceptance. We talked as we had never talked before. We cried, and, slowly, we finally began to forgive. He told me again that he really had come into the hospital room and lay down next to me but had been kicked out by the nurses, and that he had tried to call me after he had gone home, and I said, "No, Terry. It's okay. You don't have to explain. I love you. I know you did your best, and I did mine, and we both hurt each other, but it's okay. I love you, Terry, and I respect you. I want to work things out and stay with you forever." It was just the beginning, but we had started the process of truly accepting and respecting each other again.

This was only one incident of service, and already I was seeing the fruits. As I gave myself freely to greater service—to Girl Scouts, to church callings, to service for the blind and disabled workers—I found even greater rewards coming back. I would continue to serve. I would continue to give of myself.

Yes, my visions of *me* were gone, finally, and I looked around and actually sensed that the graveyard was becoming full.

Terry and the children had gone into the nearby junipers looking for more evidences of our crash. They seemed happy, talkative, excited. I saw the valley far below me where people lived normal lives. Normal meant they *all* had scars and regrets; they *all* had crashed one time or another. I wouldn't kid myself about this: *everybody* suffers, *everybody* fails. The world is a big place, and being normal means different things to different people. But I wouldn't strive to be normal anymore; I would strive to be happy through loving and sharing honestly. We either follow the thing that gives us happiness and peace, or we suffer. And no other success compensates for the loss of peace within ourselves. No rewards, no praise, no honors of man can compensate for those moments, and eventual years, of stark emptiness within.

I had learned on the other side what truly brings joy, but since then I had grown complacent from time to time, forgetting what I had learned and causing new suffering for myself and others. Could it be, if I were not careful, that one day I would read these words and wonder where they came from and how I knew them? Could I fall again? It's frightening how weak we can be, how prone to error. It can almost make us give up.

Almost.

I sat on the rock where I had screamed at God: "How dare you leave me like this! How dare you abandon me!" An awesome, humbling power had come over me, showing me the presumption of my words. I had lifted myself up to the status of the unerring one in accusing him of falling short. And I had been reminded, powerfully, of the immovability of God. He had remained constant; it was I who had wandered. And then I had prayed the most heartfelt prayer of my life and immediately received an answer in Terry's miraculous survival and our descent down the mountain. I learned that God never falls short. And just as important, I learned that he will do all in his power to protect us from our own shortcomings. He had warned me a dozen times not to go on that flight, but I had not heeded the voice. Then, after the crash, it was only a few hours later that I was given the greatest gift imaginable in the fullness of his matchless love.

His love never left.

The only prevention I know for human error is found in God. The only cure for sin and its consequences is found in his forgiveness and love. And so I pray to remember him, to remember to follow him, and to seek him when I forget. Everything I know is nothing compared to a single impression from God. Whether it comes as a voice of warning or as a whisper of approval, it is the same; it is the voice of one who cares.

I stood on the rock and looked at the scene. Scraps of metal, sheared rocks, and broken brush scattered the mountainside. My children's voices came from beyond the low trees. They had found something. Terry's voice answered them, happy, full of life. All other voices were silenced now. Even the mountain was quiet. And in it all I distinctly heard the voice of God again, a gentle, comforting voice. And I heard it in the voices of my family. Terry and I were together, and now we could create a world of our own, the world of our family, and let it grow within the sound of this gentle voice forever.